MW01154943

FAITH AND FIRE

# Elijah

## for Teen Girls

# PRISCILLA SHIRER

Lifeway Press®
Nashville, Tennessee

Published by Lifeway Press® • ©2021 Priscilla Shirer

ISBN 978-1-0877-4277-9
Item 005831695
Dewey decimal classification: 221.92
Subject heading: FAITH / ELIJAH, PROPHET / BIBLE. O.T. 1 KINGS—STUDY AND TEACHING

To order additional copies of this resource, write Lifeway Resources Customer Service; One Lifeway Plaza; Nashville, TN 37234-0113; Fax orders to 615.251.5933; call toll-free 800.458.2772; email orderentry@lifeway.com; order online at Lifeway.com.

Printed in the United States of America.

Lifeway Resources,
One Lifeway Plaza, Nashville, TN 37234-0152

## EDITORIAL TEAM, LIFEWAY STUDENT PUBLISHING

**Ben Trueblood**
Director, Student Ministry

**John Paul Basham**
Manager, Student Ministry Publishing

**Karen Daniel**
Editorial Team Leader

**Amanda Mejias**
Content Editor

**Morgan Hawk**
Production Editor

**Amy Lyon &**
**Stephanie Salvatore**
Graphic Designers

## EDITORIAL TEAM, LIFEWAY WOMEN PUBLISHING

**Becky Loyd**
Director, Lifeway Women

**Tina Boesch**
Manager, Lifeway Women Bible Studies

**Sarah Doss**
Editorial Project Leader, Lifeway Women Bible Studies

**Lawrence Kimbrough**
Content Editor

**Lindsey Bush**
Production Editor

**Lauren Ervin**
Graphic Designer

# Contents

# ABOUT THE AUTHOR

Whether in packed-out arenas or intimate Bible study group settings, Priscilla Shirer's influence has been steady and trusted. For more than twenty years her voice has resonated with raw power and unapologetic clarity to teach God's Word. Through her speaking ministry, best-selling books and Bible studies, or even on a movie screen, her primary ambition is clear—to lift up Jesus and equip His children to live victoriously.

Priscilla has been married to Jerry Shirer for twenty-one years. Together they lead Going Beyond Ministries, which exists to serve believers across the spectrum of the church. To date, the ministry has released more than a dozen video-driven studies for women and teens on a myriad of biblical characters (like Jonah and Gideon), as well as topical studies on *Discerning the Voice of God*, *The Armor of God*, and others. Priscilla has also written a fiction series called *The Prince Warriors*, in addition to award-winning books like *Fervent* and *The Resolution for Women*.

She and her family make their home near Dallas, Texas, where between writing and studying, Priscilla spends her days trying to clean up after (and satisfy the appetites of) her three rapidly growing teenage sons.

# INTRODUCTION

**IT'S BEEN A LONG TIME COMING.**

It was 2014 when I first started studying and teaching on the life and ministry of Elijah. After sharing parts of his narrative in bits and pieces, I knew I had to write about him one day. Little did I know the resource you're holding in your hands would take another seven years to materialize.

The reasons are many. Several other projects elbowed their way in, taking priority and pushing this one to the background. The busyness of my sons' lives and my involvement with them accelerated exponentially as they blossomed into young manhood. But most of the delay came from a number of unexpected, back-to-back tragedies (I'll tell you about them soon), each of which pushed the pause button on my life, forcing me to sit still for long stretches of emotional and physical recovery.

Before any of this happened, I'd felt compelled to start keeping a journal specifically for the purpose of chronicling my own spiritual journey—keeping track of God's faithfulness, recording my raw conversations with Him, tracing the often imperceptible shifts that His Spirit was working in me at the time. I'm so glad I did. Because while I'll never know my Father's reasons for all these delays—or for the losses, hurts, and challenges that precipitated them—I do know they were, at least in part, for you.

In flipping back through those handwritten entries, reliving the many things that God reframed and refreshed in my heart, I couldn't help noticing how His work in me had added layers of heartfelt depth that would've been missing from these lessons if I'd stayed on my earlier timetable. In His providence all these delays have become detours, aligning you and me in this current season of our lives. I'm convinced God has infused this work with a power that only comes through brokenness, weakness, and struggle. And I'm praying the proof of this holy impact is somehow reflected on each page—that you don't only learn something but experience something.

A renewed faith. A fresh fire.

Our world, more than ever, is longing for the sons and daughters of God to arise in the spirit of Elijah. That's why I think this might just be the perfect time for our paths to cross here, so that God can comfort you, strengthen you, encourage you, and prepare you for the Mount Carmels that lie ahead.

Welcome, my friend—I've been waiting for you. And it's been a long time coming.

*Priscilla Shirer*

# Gilead

## THE STARTING POINT

 **Faith:** Committing to God's Process

# The Start of a Process

*Right here at the very beginning of our Bible study, I want you to know one of the beautiful things to expect as we study together over the next seven sessions. I believe that as we meet together and unfold the pages of Scripture, you are going to see the beauty of an almighty, covenant-keeping God.*

*He is the God of Abraham, Isaac, and Jacob. He is the same yesterday, today, and forevermore. His plan for your redemption surpasses all time and history. He is an omnipresent, omniscient God.*

*I pray you will see through this study that He wants to interact with one individual. He wants to be seen by one individual. He wants to be heard and He wants to be experienced by one.*

*That one individual is you.*

*He wants to be seen by you, and He wants you to hear and experience Him. That's why He has brought you to this very moment.*

*So whatever reservations you might have—whatever cares and concerns you have about your ability to know and hear from God in a fresh and personal way—lay those all down at the feet of Jesus right now.*

*Open up your heart. Open up your hands. And let's get ready to meet with God.*

## Press Play

Everybody wants the Mount _____. We want the flashy display of God's _____ in our lives.

And yet in the shadows of these magnificent events is a _____. There's always a _____.

We've got to be _____ to go through the process.

Are you willing to do _____ _____ _____ to get _____ _____ _____?

## Discuss

First and Second Kings contain a series of tragedies and the failures of king after king. God's people were divided and turning their backs against each other. It shows a time of idolatry where it wasn't just tolerated and celebrated, it was legislated.

Now, let's meet Elijah.

**Read 1 Kings 17:1. Write down the name of the king that Elijah approached in this verse.**

*What did Elijah unapologetically declare before this king?*

Before we move further into this text, it is important for you to know that the name Elijah means "Yahweh is God." Which means that before Elijah ever said one word, just the mention of his name was enough for people to know where he stood.

*What's your reputation? What are you known for when you aren't around?*

Scholars are unsure of how Elijah was allowed to be in the presence of the king. But we know that it was a divine appointment given to Elijah by God, and he was probably surrounded by the king's men. Elijah's life was most likely in jeopardy.

Normally, when prophets or other people would approach the king, they wanted to simply pacify him in order to preserve their own lives (1 Kings 22:13), but Elijah was unapologetically bold. He made it clear to King Ahab that His allegiance was pledged to the one true God.

*Describe what it might look like for someone today to declare "the Lord is God" in our culture (maybe at school or on social media).*

*What do we do when something asks for our allegiance or goes against our allegiance to God?*

When I think about allegiance, I think about embassies. Did you know there are American embassies situated all over the world in many countries? Behind the walls and gates of each American embassy in those foreign environments, the laws and policies of the United States reign. The embassy doesn't change and adapt or forgo American laws just because it is located on foreign soil. It is standing in a physical location, but it's commitment and allegiance is pledged elsewhere.

*An **EMBASSY** is the location of an ambassador who serves and represents his home country in a foreign land.*

No matter where you find yourself standing and no matter how foreign the soil may be or how different it is compared to the heart of God, remember that you are an embassy for the kingdom of heaven. You represent God right where He has placed you.

***Name some areas in your life where God has called you to be His ambassador.***

# Press Play

Then he said to King Ahab, Yahweh _____.

Here's how God was going to remind Ahab that He alone is alive: "There shall be neither _____ nor rain these years, except by my _____."

Not only was the drought a judgment against the people's _____, but it was also a specific indictment against the _____ of Baal.

We can have the courage to rise up in the _____ of Elijah, and to make sure we are God's mouthpiece in this _____.

*What kind of relationships or material things does our culture count on to sustain us?*

*How does knowing that our God is alive change the way we live for Him?*

# DAY ONE
## The Real Deal

*"After you have suffered for a little while, the God of all grace, who called you to His eternal glory in Christ, will Himself perfect, confirm, strengthen, and establish you."*

**1 PETER 5:10**

I was scrolling mindlessly through my Instagram® feed one day when a particular image snagged my attention. Sort of grossed me out, to tell you the truth, peeking out from underneath my paused thumb.

Half of the image showed a beautifully poised, perfectly arched ballerina's foot. Smooth, elegant, and dainty. So pretty. So precise.

But then—the *other* side.

This other side told a much different story. The real story.

Directly next to the dancer's lovely, shapely right foot was her *other* foot. Her *bare* foot. Without its ballet slipper. And the contrast was visibly striking. Whole nails were missing. Several of the knuckles, swollen red, were bandaged, blistered, or bleeding. Fragments of old, stained gauze remained stuck to oozing sores. Knobs of contorted, misshapen bones bulged grotesquely beneath the skin.

And along with the picture ran the following caption, or words to this effect:

**EVERYONE WANTS THE GLORY,
BUT FEW ARE WILLING TO PAY THE
PRICE REQUIRED TO GET IT.**

Well, ain't that the truth.

We want the highlight reel, not the practice session. Not the years of hard work. Not the consistent pattern of sacrifice. Not the going over and over again of the same, repeated steps and movements.

> *"No discipline seems enjoyable at the time, but painful. Later on, however, it yields the peaceful fruit of righteousness to those who have been trained by it."*
>
> **HEBREWS 12:11, CSB**

The stretching. The soreness. The getting out of bed on cold, sleepy mornings. The slow, slow walk of patience, whatever it takes to get it right.

> *Have you ever had an experience on social media or at school where something seems perfect on the surface but doesn't reveal the whole truth? Describe it below.*

Truth be told, when we scroll through our social media feeds, we only want to see the ballet slipper. It's prettier and more palatable. The worn parts, the beat-up parts, douse the wildfire of our romantic imagination. Reality is too much for us to deal with. A close look at the hours of preparation, the years of hard work, and the grueling cost required to get there are not what we came to see. So we conveniently ignore that part.

If we're honest with ourselves and each other, that's how we tend to read the Bible, too.

Several years ago I took on the task of reading the entire Bible in a year. Frankly, I found it a bit overwhelming. Yet I distinctly remember, when I came to Elijah's narrative in 1 Kings that year, how I felt completely consumed by the startling boldness of his faith, especially the one, big highlight that stands out from his story: *Mount Carmel.*

> *Go ahead and turn to 1 Kings 18:19-39. (It's a pretty sizable portion of Scripture. But exciting. Lots of action. You'll love it.) As you're reading, list in the sidebar all the elements from this holy encounter that demonstrate the prophet's faith, courage, and commitment to prayer.*

As I was reading, the Holy Spirit seemed to shine a spotlight on the encounters leading up to Mount Carmel. They tell us Elijah didn't just show up out of thin air knowing exactly what to do and exactly how to do it. All that faith, all that courage, all that boldness and confidence in prayer—all that fire!—didn't just happen.

What stood out to you the most while reading the Mount Carmel story?

_____

_____

_____

_____

_____

_____

_____

_____

_____

_____

_____

_____

_____

_____

_____

_____

This moment of biblical proportions, high atop Mount Carmel, followed a much less public process that God had begun in him years before—a process that is already happening in you as well, which your loving Father will continue to develop throughout this study—a progression of development that I hope you'll begin to recognize and value more than ever before.

I'm assuming you're here with me in these pages because we both want what Elijah had.

**We want:**
- faith, courage, and boldness,
- a prayer life that pushes back the darkness,
- character that possesses an unflinching backbone, and
- a holy conviction that doesn't bow to popular opinion.

**We want to be:**
- filled with the fullness of God's Spirit and power,
- brave enough to speak truth to authority with love and grace,
- singularly focused, inspiring others' allegiance to the one true God, and
- people who leave behind a lasting impact on future generations.

*If you could have just two things from these lists for your own life, what would they be?*

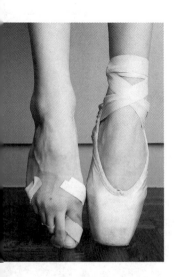

These are incredibly noble aspirations. But the question for us remains:

### ARE WE WILLING TO DO WHAT ELIJAH DID TO GET WHAT ELIJAH GOT?

Hear me, sister, and hear me good. The process of pursuing Christ will not be easy. In fact, I can assure you, it will cost you something.

But still, it will all be worth it.

# Just Like Me

---

*"Friends, why are you doing this?*
*We too are only human, like you."*

**ACTS 14:15a, NIV**

---

**Turn to James 5:17 in your own Bible. In the space below, write down the opening phrase—just through the first comma or so.**

I don't know if what I'm about to say will come as a surprise, and I don't want to spoil some of the lessons we'll study down the line. But as a bit of a preview for what the Bible is going to show us about the things Elijah faced in life and how he dealt with them, prepare for these realities:

- We're going to see Elijah hungry, tired, and irritable.
- We're going to see Elijah discouraged and hopeless.
- We're going to see Elijah doubtful and insecure.

In other words, we are going to see Elijah as human.

Yes, the great prophet Elijah had his emotional tailspins. *We'll see them.* The great prophet Elijah was an expert at wallowing in self-pity. *We'll see it.* The great prophet Elijah failed and flailed and needed God the same way we fail and flail and need God ourselves. *Get ready to see that, too.* Even after the adrenaline rush of watching God's fire fall from heaven at Mount Carmel, and then actively participating in bringing his enemies to a fitting end, Elijah crashed into an abyss of exhaustion and fatigue. And fear. And paranoia. He ran. He was done.

So while Elijah is an example for us, he is not an exception to us. We must resist our tendency to idolize him and other biblical heroes like him. None of the biblical heroes were intended to be an exception; they are all meant to be examples to us of what happens when an ordinary life intersects with

> *James wrote to a community of Jewish Christians who were being persecuted for their faith and as a result had been "scattered abroad" (1:1, NKJV) out of Jerusalem. They were enduring intense external persecution along with internal battles of the flesh—anger, vengeance, and the temptation to sin.*

an extraordinary God. Prepare yourself to look at Elijah this way, and then see what the Holy Spirit reveals to you in the process.

Based on some of the "coming attractions" that I told you we can expect to see in Elijah's life, let me ask you to be introspective for a moment. In what specific ways do you deal with:

- Insecurity?

- Irritability?

- Discouragement?

- Loss of perspective?

*How does it encourage you to realize someone as epic as Elijah could feel and battle with some of these same things?*

Here's how it helps me. It tells me Elijah's limitations, weaknesses, and emotional quirks didn't scare God off or disqualify him from serving God in a mighty way.

God knew all these tendencies in Elijah. He factored all of them into the unique plan He'd designed for Elijah's life. He didn't ignore His prophet's needs and worries. He worked with them; He made use of them in showing His care for Elijah, as well as showing what He can accomplish in each of us despite our human imperfections.

*Looking at the previous paragraph, underline the portions that encourage you to free yourself from feelings of self-condemnation or uselessness.*

And do you know what I see, as you sit there? I see a lot of Elijah in you.

"Our biblical heroes are examples of what happens when an ordinary life intersects with an extraordinary God."

#ELIJAHBIBLESTUDY

# These Are the Days of Elijah

*"You have observed the statutes of Omri and all the practices of Ahab's house; you have followed their traditions. Therefore I will give you over to ruin and your people to derision; you will bear the scorn of nations."*

**MICAH 6:16, NIV**

My nephew Kamden is a five-year-old ball of human fire, filled with more energy and precocious mischievousness than maybe any kid I've ever met. The fourth of five children, he is constantly trying to press the limits, to push past the boundaries. If not for the watchful oversight of his parents—my brother Jonathan and his wife, Kanika—there'd be no barrier between himself and the dangers of, say, a swimming pool, a crowded intersection, a threatening animal. You get the picture? This is the reason why one of Kamden's frequent locations is right smack-dab in the middle of his father's lap, being lovingly and securely held down for his own protection.

Sometimes, though, I've watched Jonathan let him go—not because he didn't want to protect his son, but because he decided in the moment that Kamden would learn better through painful experience. Not enough to injure him, but enough to teach him this valuable lesson: *My father knows best.*

Our relationship with our heavenly Father is much the same. Many times, in order to keep us protected, He holds us close. He hems us in. But other times, still motivated by that same great love, He releases us to our own demands.

He lets go. And we learn the hard way.

In 1 Kings 17, as Elijah first comes into view, the sense we get from Scripture is that God had released the nation to the consequences of their duplicitous choices. Sort of like my nephew Kamden, the Israelites had stiffened their necks against God's protective authority.

Over the course of eight decades in Israel, spanning the reigns of six different kings, the God-honoring families who once esteemed Him had incrementally relaxed their commitments. They'd departed from the singular worship of Yahweh. They'd welcomed idolatrous activity into their lives as an accepted practice.

Now Ahab, who was the king of Israel when Elijah emerged onto the scene "walked in all the way of Jeroboam" (1 Kings 16:26). This comment compels us to discover what former King Jeroboam did.

**After discussions with his advisors, what did Jeroboam set up in the northern cities (1 Kings 12:28-29)?**

**Whom did he install as religious leaders there (1 Kings 12:31)?**

*Jeroboam's actions were a flagrant example of* **SYNCRETISM.** *(SINK-re-tism), the practice of absorbing conflicting religious views into one cosmopolitan belief system, until all roads lead to God, and nothing really means anything.*

Jeroboam combined the worship of Yahweh with idolatry. He didn't forbid Israel's allegiance to God, but he made it divided. And whenever loyalties are divided, that's where decline always begins.

Ruling in this way—in "the way of Jeroboam"—was a common descriptor for all the kings of Israel. But for Ahab, it was just the beginning. He considered what the previous kings had done in dishonoring God "a trivial thing" (1 Kings 16:31). Ahab "did evil in the sight of the LORD more than all who were before him" (v. 30).

For instance, he built an altar to Baal for the Israelites to worship—not in addition to God, but in place of God (v. 32). He added to this blasphemy by making an image of Asherah, the goddess mother of Baal (v. 33). Then in complete disregard for the law of God, he married a pagan wife, Jezebel, daughter of a pagan king. She insisted the worship of Baal become the sum total of Israel's religious life, effectively criminalizing the worship of Yahweh. Israelite culture was no longer divided but now demonic and degenerate.

The spiritual indifference and negligence of all the kings of Israel since Solomon had been offensive to God. Year after year. Decade after decade. But the sharpness of Ahab's departure from worship of the one true God grieved the Lord even more. And at this point of the downhill spiral, God did what fathers sometimes have to do.

*He let go.*

And like it or not, God does so even now. The sad reality is that our current culture is experiencing some of the same effects of this divine relinquishing.

> **Read Romans 1:18-32. I know it's a tough passage, and a lengthy one. But the gravity of it is too critical to shortcut. As you read, underline in your Bible anything that stands out as being particularly convicting to you.**

Even in this difficult reading, don't overlook God's desire to comfort, to *hold us close.* In verse 20, we see a loving God taking the initiative to make known His invisible presence, to establish relationship with people. He doesn't want to be hidden and unknown.

But we are simultaneously confronted. We see Him *let us go.* When people foolishly declare there is no God, or when they dishonor Him by refusing to acknowledge Him or give Him due reverence, He eventually lets go. When people hate the things God has called good or love the things He's called evil, He finally just lets them have what they want, as well as the consequences that come with it.

> **Zero in on the verses from Romans 1 reprinted in the margin. Underline each place where it says "God gave them over." Circle what they experience after He gave them over.**

As children of God—saved, redeemed, and forgiven—the status of our relationship with Him never changes, just as Kamden's relationship to his daddy never changes. But it doesn't mean our *experience* with Him won't change if we persist in refusing to honor Him. He will sometimes choose tough, letting-go love as the best option for reminding us that the ingredients we're mixing into our lives are a recipe for disaster.

These were the days of Elijah. Days of experiencing God's letting go. But just when Israel was spiraling downward, God was stirring up a representative in the rugged mountains of Gilead who would call His people back.

Elijah was coming.

*"Therefore God gave them over in the lusts of their hearts to impurity, so that their bodies would be dishonored among them" (v. 24).*

*"For this reason God gave them over to degrading passions" (v. 26a).*

*"And just as they did not see fit to acknowledge God any longer, God gave them over to a depraved mind" (v. 28a).*

# The Process of Preparation

*"Elijah the Tishbite, who was of the settlers of Gilead ..."*

**1 KINGS 17:1a**

Let's dig into 1 Kings 17. This is the first mention of Elijah in Scripture. And while we don't learn a lot about his background from the opening verse, we at least learn this:

- Elijah was a _____.

- His hometown was in an area called _____.

- And his first allegiance was to _____.

The exact location of *Tishbe*, despite being home to one of the greatest figures in all the Bible, cannot really be identified. Geologists and archaeologists have never been able to pinpoint it with any degree of accuracy. But *Gilead* comes with a bit more documentation.

Gilead was hill country, covered with dense forests and wild undergrowth. It was remote and uncivilized. Even its name—*Gilead*—means "rocky" or "rugged."

That's where Elijah was from. And that's who Elijah was. A mountain man. Elijah wasn't groomed in the sophisticated manners and etiquette of the city. Elijah lacked classical education and social polish. He wasn't brought up in echelons of society where he could earn the kinds of credentials and connections that paved his way to success.

Scholars believe he likely tended sheep on the heights of those lonely, uneven hillsides in Gilead.[1] It's where he learned to value and endure endless stretches of solitude and silence. It's where he had time to grow into a muscular, sinewy man with the tenacity it took to stave off predators and provide for his flocks.

Elijah came from a hard place. A rough place. An obscure place. The right place to be prepared for what God had in store for him.

*Have you ever questioned why God allowed you to go through a season of hardship or to experience a certain difficulty? How so?*

The various events and circumstances that have contributed to your life up until this point have not been accidental. They've not been wasted parts of your process, even if they were difficult, even if they excluded you from certain privileges that in your estimation could have propelled you forward faster. Even the evil that's been done against you by people who intended you harm has not been a total loss. This doesn't excuse their wrongdoing, of course. It doesn't minimize the real pain they've caused you. But it does add a layer of perspective and hope.

As Joseph could say, after being wrongfully treated by his brothers, after being unjustly enslaved and imprisoned in Egypt, "God meant it for good in order to bring about this present result" (Gen. 50:20).

For Elijah, the fact that he was raised in an uncivilized environment; the fact that he wasn't brought up around more cultured tastes and people; the fact that he grew up at a distance from mass civilization; the fact that he had no lineage or pedigree even worth mentioning in the Bible. There was a reason for it.

All of it set the stage for the life God had planned for him.

In Gilead.

> *"God is faithful, through whom you were called into fellowship with His Son, Jesus Christ our Lord."*
>
> **1 CORINTHIANS 1:9**

During Elijah's unrecorded years in Gilead, he somehow came to know, to *really* know, Yahweh. One way or another, while doing his tedious, mundane, lonesome work, while facing hardships we'll never know, Elijah had been exposed to influences that convinced him Jehovah wasn't just one deity among many other options. He'd developed a deep knowledge, reverence, and understanding for Yahweh's covenant with His people, a holy perspective that would form the basis for his first prophetic declaration in Scripture. This God, Israel's God, was a jealous God who had no intention of sharing His glory with man-made idols.

That's what Elijah learned in Gilead.

- In *Gilead*, where he was from.
- In *Gilead*, where his heart was formed.
- In *Gilead*, where his own personal set of trials and difficulties became the start of a process, a process of living and thinking and navigating his journey by faith.

The backside of that raw, rugged desert was God's way of bringing Elijah around to know Him in a way he would never have experienced Him otherwise. Now he was ready to declare God's word with boldness and authority.

> *Describe a time in your life when you have seen God use difficult circumstances to reveal Himself more clearly and to draw you closer to Himself?*

Elijah's whole life was about to become a clear, bold declaration of God's power and provision.

And so is yours.

Where you have come from. What you have been through.

All of it has been preparing you for the purpose He's planned next.

> *As you close today's lesson, take a few moments to thank the Lord for your journey so far. Ask Him to give you the courage to trust that He is using every part of it—even the difficult or despairing parts—to form you into His image, to focus your passions and pursuits, and to funnel you into the stream of His purposes for this generation, for future generations.*

> *"It is good for me that I was afflicted, so that I may learn Your statutes. The Law of Your mouth is better to me than thousands of gold and silver pieces. Your hands made me and fashioned me; give me understanding, so that I may learn Your commandments."*
>
> **PSALM 119:71-73**

# DAY FIVE
# Elijah Calling

Take a few minutes and look up what your name means. Write it in the space below.

*"Before I formed you in the womb I knew you,*
*And before you were born I consecrated you;*
*I have appointed you as a prophet to the nations."*

**JEREMIAH 1:5**

In biblical days, names were quite often synonymous with a person's calling and character. They signified one's reputation. The syllables of Hebrew names, like a puzzle meticulously fitted together, built layer upon layer of insight into who this person really was or was meant to be. So when Elijah first arrived in town, anyone in the vicinity would have known where his allegiance stood, simply by hearing his name.

- *El*, meaning, "God"
- *I*, meaning, "my"
- *Jah*, meaning, "Yahweh"

People who knew Elijah knew where he stood, even before they really knew him.

Elijah's first words to Ahab in 1 Kings 17:1 were sort of a pledge of allegiance, which corresponded with the meaning of his name. Turn to this verse and notice the layers:

- The LORD

- The LORD is _____

- The LORD is God of _____

- The LORD God of Israel _____

- The LORD God of Israel lives, and I have pledged my sole allegiance to Him.

*YAHWEH is the name God calls Himself. In Hebrew tradition, His name was considered too holy even to speak aloud. So in the Old Testament, where this name appears more than six thousand times, it was changed to the word Adonai, which in English versions is printed "LORD," in all capital letters.[2]*

*See "Digging Deeper, Part 1" on page 26.*

*Turn to and read Deuteronomy 29, particularly verses 16-29, where God revealed the cost to be paid by those who rejected His covenant.*

**What did Elijah say was God's impending judgment on the nation of Israel because of their rebellion?**

Based on what Elijah knew about God's covenant with His people (Deut. 29, for example), he knew Israel's rebellion deserved judgment. And despite the fact that these negative results of the people's disobedience would adversely affect Elijah too—such as the land being "unsown and unproductive" so that "no grass grows in it" (Deut. 29:23)—he was brave enough and so committed to God that he still prayed for it.

Elijah had developed such a commitment to Yahweh that he was willing to pray for His will to be done above all else, even above his own comfort.

And he was willing to speak this unbending truth to the most powerful man in the nation.

**To whom did Elijah declare God's forthcoming judgment?**

How did this guy get in here?

Scholars are unsure how Elijah ever ended up being granted an audience with King Ahab and why his life was spared when he did, especially considering the unwelcome message he came to deliver. Nothing other than the sovereignty of the Almighty God could be responsible for arranging this unimaginable appointment.

But we do know this: they understood what this meeting was about, even before the prophet opened his mouth. Elijah's name had become synonymous with his character. His God was Yahweh.

Apparently his whole life had been shaped by the meaning of his name.

So as 1 Kings 17 opens, Elijah was physically standing before a king. But his real standing—his true allegiance—was before Yahweh.

This is how you must frame your entire life. You can attend this school or that university, participate in that organization, or answer to that coach, and at the same time keep your ultimate allegiance securely situated in the one true God.

In fact, you must treat your allegiance like this if you genuinely want to honor Him. You can be standing *there*, but really be standing here with your hand over your heart before your true Lord and King.

Because when you know your name, even if you're from a nowhere place like Gilead—when you've committed yourself to the process of learning who you are, based on the truth of the One who has called you to serve and follow Him—you can stand and declare His Word in any place, in front of anybody. You can know, like Elijah did, that your God is Yahweh, that you represent the One whom no man or worldly idol can replace, remove, or redact.

As the daughter of a King, your name has been imbued with all the rights and privileges that give you access through Christ to your Father's power. Everything God has allowed you to march through in life so far has been intended to mature your faith, fortify your principles, shape your character, and cement your allegiance to Him. It's been preparing you to take your stand in that confidence.

Your identity as a believer is something you wear today. Right now. *Here* is where you stand.

> Turn to 1 Peter 2:9-10 as we prepare to close this week of study. Fill in the blanks in the sidebar with what the Bible asserts to be your identity as a believer in Christ.

This is who you are. Each one of these features—and more—is part of your given name. It's been your name from the moment you put your faith in Christ as Savior, and it will be your name for as long as you live.

Knowing your name—knowing who you are—gives you the courage to stand on the bedrock of eternal truth, to stand there in the name of the One who "called you for a righteous purpose" (Isa. 42:6, CSB).

So when Elijah set out from Gilead, tromping out of the hills toward the city, toward the throne room of Ahab, with God's Word in his mouth and God's strength pulsating in his heart, he may not have known much. But he did know what his name meant. And there he would take his stand.

I can't wait to see in the next six weeks where it takes him. And us.

**chosen:**
you are "a chosen
_____"

**royal:**
you are "a royal
_____"

**holy:**
you are "a holy
_____"

**child of God:**
you are God's own
"_____"

**proclaimer:**
made to proclaim or declare His
"_____"

**called:**
you've been called
"out of _____"

**light:**
called into His marvelous, wonderful
"_____"

# Heaven's Rain

Centuries before Elijah's prophetic ministry, Yahweh delivered the Hebrew children from brutal slavery in Egypt. As Moses led them toward their freedom in Canaan, he took great care to point out an interesting contrast between the two locations. Egypt was "where you used to sow your seed and water it ... But the land into which you are about to cross to possess it" is a land that "drinks water from the rain of heaven" (Deut. 11:10-11). The distinction between the land of their captivity and the promised land is that the first had been watered by hand, but the other would be sustained and watered by the loving and faithful hand of their Deliverer. In other words, an open heaven was a sign of God's favor and blessing on His people as they continued to submit to His authority and worship Him alone.

They had been warned, as they contemplated their future in Canaan:

> *"Beware that your hearts are not easily deceived, and that you do not turn away and serve other gods, and worship them. Otherwise, the anger of the LORD will be kindled against you, and He will shut up the sky so that there will be no rain, and the ground will not yield its produce; then you will quickly perish from the good land which the LORD is giving you."*
> **DEUTERONOMY 11:16-17**

Elijah's pronouncement of drought to King Ahab and the nation had ramifications that went beyond a simple weather forecast. It signified the judgment of Yahweh upon Israel for their rebellion and their ongoing refusal to submit to His authority. Elijah's declaration was not rooted in his own plan. He knew the Word of his God, and Elijah based his message to Ahab on the holy covenant that had been established in the wilderness.

But that's not the only thing Elijah had in mind as he prophesied the coming drought. Baal and his female cohort Asherah were recognized and worshiped as the god and goddess of fertility. It was believed that Baal also had power over rain. Storms, they thought, were in his control.

As idol worship became more widely sanctioned and practiced in Israel, then officially legislated under Ahab and Jezebel's leadership, the people of God essentially rejected Yahweh as their primary source of provision. Israel increasingly believed that these false gods controlled the weather,

> *"All the sons of Israel, seeing the fire come down and the glory of the LORD upon the house, bowed down on the pavement with their faces to the ground, and they worshiped and gave praise to the LORD, saying, 'Certainly He is good, certainly His faithfulness is everlasting.'"*
>
> **2 CHRONICLES 7:3**

the change of seasons, and, by extension, their crops' ability to yield a bountiful harvest. They began to believe that their ability to survive rested squarely in Baal's hands. The people appealed endlessly to the gods in hopes of garnering favor, thinking it ensured rain for their crops and promised success for their agrarian society.

Each month the sky withheld rain was a personal strike against the authority of Baal to control nature. As an impotent idol, he had no control whatsoever over the rain and sun. Each of the 1,200-plus days of drought and famine would remind the people that only one God held supreme authority, and their allegiance should be to Him only.

The judgments God imposed upon ancient Israel are a reminder to us that any consequences we endure today are never about the consequences alone. They are designed to reveal the weaknesses of our idols, debunk the myth of their power, and remind us that God alone is worthy of our loyalty and worship.

Whenever we anchor our significance unwisely, putting our trust in health, success, material wealth, or relationships, thereby turning them into illegitimate gods, our heavenly Father will cut them off at the knees and remind us of their insufficiency to save.

*Remember, the nation split in two after Solomon's death. The two tribes of the Southern Kingdom were known as Judah; the ten tribes of the Northern Kingdom were known as Israel.*

*"Like scarecrows in a cucumber patch, their idols cannot speak. They must be carried because they cannot walk. Do not fear them for they can do no harm—and they cannot do any good. LORD, there is no one like you. You are great; your name is great in power."*
**JEREMIAH 10:5-6, CSB**

# Cherith

## THE PART NOBODY SEES

 **Faith:** Committing to God's Process

# Preparation by Separation

*One day my niece Kelsey decided she wanted to make some homemade cookies. The problem is that she had only ever made these chocolate chip cookies with her mother's oversight. But this time she wanted to do it all by herself.*

*So Kelsey gathered all of the ingredients together and proceeded to make the cookies. As she watched the cookies bake, she realized that something wasn't right. The cookies weren't rising. They were flat as pancakes and they were burning on the bottom!*

*Kelsey's parents pulled out the ingredient list and asked her if she had missed anything. It wasn't until then that she realized she had left out the main ingredient: the flour. Upon this mistake, she decided to toss the cookies into the trash since she didn't feel like they were worth eating. But her parents said, "Oh, no! You decided you could cook them yourself, so you get to eat them."*

*Never again would she miss the main ingredient. But the flour wasn't actually the key ingredient she missed. It was her mom. Kelsey forgot she needed to depend on someone else to help her cook it the right way.*

*If you're anything like me, there have been times when you've had to "eat" something that you've "cooked" without the oversight of God. This week, God is going to remind us to have a continual state of dependence on Him through the prophet Elijah.*

# Press Play

God wants to _____ you.

Here's how you know when God is beginning to _____ you for the next season in your journey with Him. He calls you to _____ your grasp on something, someone, or someplace.

Ask the Holy Spirit to spotlight any specific ways where God is asking you to _____ from here, to get up and get out, to relocate and _____ your life in some way.

If we want the _____ that will come to us in the place of separation, then we have to be _____ to do the hard, Holy Spirit _____ work of consecrating our lives.

# Discuss

*How might God call His followers to be separated or set apart?*

*What is God asking you to separate yourself from?*

*Read 1 Kings 17:4. What did God provide for Elijah at the brook? Why is that a big deal?*

This is exciting because a drought's coming. You remember? In 1 Kings 17:1, Elijah made this pronouncement. A drought will be in full swing for three and a half years throughout the entire nation. It was going to be completely devastating and the drought was going to cause a famine so powerful that the effects of it were even going to spill over into other territories. People would be scavenging and hoarding for food, trying to find water that is increasingly difficult to find. But not Elijah.

Because here at Cherith, in the place of separation and solitude, God has promised to sustain him. And the same is true for you. Not only does God want to separate you, He wants to sustain you.

*When God calls us to be separated, what might we lack or need?*

*In a time when you were in need, how did you experience God sustaining you?*

When you feel a little bit lonely, He's going to show you what it's like when He becomes your friend. When you're tired, you're going to finally know what it's like when God becomes your strength. When you're hungry, you'll experience Him, not just in the testimony of somebody else that you've heard before, but finally you'll know what it's like when He's the bread of life. When you're thirsty, He becomes a river of living water. When you're insecure, feeling a little bit intimidated, you'll see what it's like when He becomes your security. And when you're empty, you'll see what it's like when your God fills you up. He wants to sustain you. Give Him the opportunity to show you what it's like to be nourished by God and God alone.

*What does God's provision reveal about His character?*

It's in those moments of separation where we not only experience the provision, but the provider and sustainer, Himself. And right there at the brook, Elijah was being reminded of who his sustainer is.

Because at this point in the story, God's people by and large were trusting in the rain as their source. They were looking to the rain god Baal to sustain them. Therefore, He takes Elijah aside without any rain and without any external outside provision so he could learn what it's like to be sustained by God and God alone because Elijah will be alone again.

Make no mistake. He's going to be standing on Mount Carmel, surrounded by those who are antagonistic to the one, true God and surrounded by thousands of his countrymen. But even with all of those people standing around, he's still going to be all by himself because he's going to be the only one in that moment, standing for righteousness, representing an unapologetic covenant, keeping God in the midst of a crowd.

Elijah had to become acquainted with the rhythms of grace that keep one steadfast and immovable and always abounding in the work of the Lord. He needed to have some backbone before he could withstand the isolating spotlight of Carmel. And so do you.

Do you understand that in an increasingly post-Christian culture, we're going to have to have some backbone? This is not going to be a time for wimps. We're going to have to know what it's like to be so sustained and at peace and comfortable in our relationship with God that even when we're in a crowd, if we have to stand alone, we can do it with boldness and with confidence, knowing that if our God is for us, then it doesn't matter who is against us. Separate yourself and watch God sustain you, build into you an inner security based on His spirit that you would not otherwise have, an inner strength from which you can draw in times to come.

# Press Play

God wants to _____ you.

According to Ephesians 3:20-21, God does exceedingly, abundantly, above and beyond anything that you can _____ or _____.

God wants to _____ you.

Elijah had no idea that while he was being obedient in _____, he was actually being _____ from something he didn't even know he was in danger of.

# Discuss

*When have you experienced God protect and shield you from a dangerous situation?*

*How does His provision and protection encourage us to obey His calling?*

# DAY ONE

# Separation Anxiety

---

*"Go, my people, enter your rooms and close your doors behind you. Hide for a little while until the wrath has passed."*

**ISAIAH 26:20, CSB**

---

Before the year 2020, most of us had never heard the phrase "social distancing." Then within what seemed like a matter of days, we went from meeting with friends at local coffee shops to wearing face masks, quarantining in our homes, and using technology as our only means of school.

Turns out though, this idea of setting oneself apart has long been part of God's process in developing His people for usefulness and impact. Jesus demonstrated it Himself, enduring forty days of solitude before entering into public ministry (Matt. 4:1). Throughout His earthly life, He would often "slip away to the wilderness" (Luke 5:16) to be alone with God, usually "in the early morning, while it was still dark" (Mark 1:35). Socially distant—before the rest of us even knew social distance was a thing.

As far back as 1 Kings 17, we see Yahweh prescribe for Elijah a season of separation as a necessary stop on the prophet's journey to spiritual maturity and victory.

*"Go away from here and turn eastward, and hide yourself by the brook Cherith, which is east of the Jordan."*

**1 KINGS 17:3**

> *Read 1 Kings 17:2-4 in your Bible. Focusing on verse 3 in the margin, what are the three actions that God required Elijah to take?*

> *As you begin this week of study, ask the Holy Spirit to give you clarity in responding to the following three related questions:*
>
> *1. What have you sensed God asking you to leave or go away from that's been a customary part of your life?*

*2. What direction have you felt the Spirit turning you toward?*

*3. Here's the final and most important question. Have you obeyed the Holy Spirit's conviction in these matters? If not, what do you think has kept you from it?*

While Cherith's precise GPS coordinates remain a mystery to modern explorers, its dynamics do not. All the land "east of the Jordan" was rugged and unkempt. It was known for its long stretches of lonely wasteland, broken only by thin streams of trickling water here and there, like the brook called simply, singularly, Cherith.

**CHERITH** *is a place name meaning "cutting" or "ditch."*[1]

No one now knows for sure where this narrow stream (pronounced KEER-ith) was located. But Elijah knew. Concealed in the hills, this rivulet where God had called him to isolate himself was a place of pervasive silence and widespread solitude. This secluded spot away from everything was the perfect place for God to accomplish the next stage of His intended work in the life of His servant.

*Consider some of the dynamics Elijah would be leaving behind—within the palace, for example, where he'd just begun his public ministry as a prophet of Yahweh—and the stark contrast Cherith presented him. Write some of your observations below.*

Elijah's calling for the time being would not keep him in proximity of the palace or amid the throbbing heart of the masses. Instead, he was being ordered to isolate himself, out where he'd not be able to consult with or depend on any other human, to simply be alone with his God. Here he'd need to entrust the results of his ministry to the One who'd called him to Ahab's court in the first place, and who just as clearly had called him away now into the next leg of the process.

*When God removes us from a season that's been populated with many people and relationships into one that's marked by solitude, it can be unsettling. Why might such an abrupt shift sometimes be necessary in adjusting our perspectives, pruning our pride, and reorienting our priorities?*

Mind if I just speak to you from my own heart and experience for a second? Everybody's life is different; I understand that. But as I look back on mine, I see where at every turn, every time God has been preparing me to tackle a fresh challenge or to move into a new spiritual place with Him, the process He's chosen has almost always begun with a stop in "Cherith"—a season of life that I perceived at the time to be undesirably obscure, isolating, unproductive, and relatively mundane.

Truth be told, I haven't always complied quickly or easily with wherever God was sending me—at least not voluntarily, as Elijah appeared to do. God has often needed to push me, closing doors in one direction, lighting my path to another, severing and resetting relationships, then diverting me toward Cherith and the disciplines and values He knew it would develop in me: a renewed passion for prayer, a fresh hunger for His voice, and a clearer focus on His priorities.

I haven't always understood why this "Cherith" or part of the process is necessary. It's sometimes seemed to me like a waste of weeks, months, and years, away from the work He's been calling me to do—work that seems a lot more important to me than the little I appeared to be accomplishing while at Cherith. But just as Elijah apparently needed to learn, I'm not as necessary to the greater work of God, as much as the greater work of God is necessary in me.

The Cherith is where He keeps teaching me this. And whenever He's wanted to reshape and refocus me in areas where my flesh has begun to take control, or just to prepare me for the next stage of my journey with Him, He whispers:

*Priscilla, My daughter, trust Me. Go away from where you've been. Cut unnecessary passions, ambitions, and people that are dividing your affections and allegiance. Turn your energy and attention in a new direction, toward new goals that I will show you. Hide yourself there, and rest until I release you.*

Pay attention when you sense God's Spirit speaking to you in this way. Notice they're the same three things He said to Elijah:

1. "GO AWAY FROM HERE." When the Spirit begins to whisper this directive, you'll sense a rise of conviction in your soul about a current aspect of your life, compelling you to leave behind a habit, an ambition, perhaps even a relationship you may not want to leave.

2. "TURN." As you obey and separate yourself, He'll begin to show you a new direction, interest, or goal to pivot toward. This clarity might not be immediate, but He will slowly begin reorienting your heart and hands in a new direction. When He does, go that way. Turn that way.

3. "HIDE." Fully immerse yourself in the lessons He wants to teach you and the spiritual disciplines He longs to renew in you. Fully separate yourself from the idols pulling back against your commitment to Him and making you halfhearted. Then press into the new internal postures and external dynamics that Cherith requires. Rest here until He determines it's time to release you.

> *In thinking about these three steps, do you currently see the Lord dealing with you in any specific way? Which step? Which aspects of your relationship with Him point to this?*

Elijah, unbeknownst to him, was being prepared for a public showdown that would demand a level of courage, conviction, and inner fortitude he did not yet possess. And Cherith was one of the places where God would produce it in him.

Don't despise the solitude of Cherith, sister. The spiritual power you desire (and will soon require) cannot be cultivated any other place.

# My Provider

*"You will drink from the brook ..."*

**1 KINGS 17:4**

When my boys were younger, we'd often take walks behind one of my best friend's houses, crossing her back acreage until we came to a thick cove of trees. Once past the timberline, we felt as though we'd entered another world.

Few things are much more naturally adventurous than trekking through the woods with three little boys, climbing over rocks, balancing yourself on fallen trees, listening for sounds, looking for bugs. But most of all, we enjoyed the part of the property where a small brook ran through. Sometimes after a heavy rain, it would be filled with water that danced around the rocks, rushing downstream where it emptied into a larger creek. At other times though, particularly in summer, when rain in Texas plays hard to get, the stream bed would be as dry as a cotton ball.

That's the thing about brooks. They aren't consistent. You can't count on them. Brooks are sometime-y. If it doesn't rain, they don't hold any water.

That's the thing about Cherith too. It was just a little unreliable brook. A brook that needed rain in order to thrive. And the rain, as you know, was ending. God had told Elijah to say there'd be "neither dew nor rain" in these parts for a number of years (1 Kings 17:1). So the effect on this brook and its lone inhabitant was inescapable. What would happen after Elijah had been at Cherith for more than a few days? Without rain?

That's what makes Elijah's yielded obedience to God's instruction about hiding himself at Cherith even more amazing. He obeyed even with this risky reality in mind. Surrendering to Yahweh's assignment would've been more understandable if God had told him to go hang out beside a *river*. A river could resist the effects of drought much longer. But the combination of famine and an unpredictable brook, along with God's directive to go hide there for an extended period of time, must have sounded like a really bad idea. And yet the prophet obeyed.

I believe his unreserved obedience was primarily prompted by one thing:

**Read 1 Kings 17:3-4a, printed below. Circle God's promise to Elijah.**

"Go away from here and turn eastward, and hide yourself by the brook Cherith, which is east of the Jordan. And it shall be that you will drink from the brook [wadi] ..." _____

**Now write this promise verbatim below.**

*Some versions of 1 Kings 17:4 may use the word* **WADI,** *the Hebrew term for* **"BROOK."** *Wadis, which are numerous in the Middle East, are rocky watercourses that are dry except for rainy seasons.*[2]

Just so you know, I've repeated this promise throughout your entire devotional today. It's at the top of today's lesson, and you'll see it again and again. My hope is that its truth will nestle deeply inside your soul, quieting any anxiety you may feel about your next experience at Cherith and filling you with a sense of peace about it when it comes.

Sister, don't skim over the spectacular revelation to be gleaned from just this tiny sliver of Scripture. God intentionally hid His beloved prophet near a water source that was at best seasonal. In fact, we'll notice it soon enough in our study next week. When God was ready to move Elijah on to the next part of the process, this *wadi* did what *wadis* do. It dried up.

God in His sovereignty knew this would happen. *Before He sent him.* Yet throughout the entire time that Elijah obediently hid there, surrendering to a season of seclusion and training, of waiting and hiding, God told Elijah not to worry about where his water would come from. The God of oceans made him a promise: "You will drink of the brook." You will.

Your needs will be met. You will be refreshed.

No question. No matter. No ifs, ands, or buts.

Pause and absorb this truth for a moment. Your new *position* at Cherith has come with a *promise.* A promise of God's care and provision. Thank Him for this, even while perhaps you sit there today beside a brook in your own life that's looking mighty dry right now.

*In the margin, write how you intend to change your attitude, approach, and actions, in light of the following promises:*

- "I will never desert you, nor will I ever abandon you" (Heb. 13:5).

- "The Lord will rescue me from every evil attack and will bring me safely to his heavenly kingdom" (2 Tim. 4:18a, NIV).

- "God is able to make all grace overflow to you, so that, always having all sufficiency in everything, you may have an abundance for every good deed" (2 Cor. 9:8).

- "If we ask anything according to His will, He hears us" (1 John 5:14b).

- "If any of you lacks wisdom, let him ask of God, who gives to all generously and without reproach, and it will be given to him" (Jas. 1:5).

- "Sustain me as you promised, and I will live; do not let me be ashamed of my hope. Sustain me so that I can be safe and always be concerned about your statutes" (Ps. 119:116-117, CSB).

These are just a few of the promises that give you confidence, like Elijah, to yield to God's work at your Cherith when you see it beginning to run dry. The unpredictable people and circumstances in your life will not be able to unsettle you nearly as much when you're resting in God's Word that says, "Your peace and provision are not rooted in the undependable things around you. Your hope is embedded in something else. In Someone else."

"You will drink of the brook."

God will provide. God will supply. When you're going through times of *separation* from your usual surroundings, remember you are not separated from the One who's promised to sustain you where He's placed you. Your available resources may feel shaky and uncertain, but if He sent you there, then He will sustain you there. He will not fail to "supply all your needs according to His riches in glory in Christ Jesus" (Phil. 4:19).

Yahweh's promise—"You will drink of the brook"—was designed to teach Elijah the same lesson your fickle Cherith is intended to teach you—a truth that Elijah would need to know without any doubt before he ever stepped foot on Mount Carmel. His real source of sustenance was not the inadequate resources of the brook Cherith, any more than if it had been the vast, robust waters of the Mediterranean Sea. The ultimate source of Elijah's provision was God Himself.

*Underline the last line of the previous paragraph. Then fill in the blanks of the statement below:*

• *God is reminding me that my _____ source of _____ is Him.*

Yahweh allows the stuff of Earth to be lacking in its ability to fulfill us so that we have no choice but to look to Him for our ultimate satisfaction.

- When you are lonely, God is your friend.
- When you are tired, God is your strength.
- When you are hungry, _____ is your Bread of life.
- When you are dry, _____ is your Living Water.
- When you are insecure, _____ is your confidence.
- When you are empty, _____ is your fulfillment.

If God has placed you alongside a brook like this, in a dry season like this—a wadi that hasn't been reliable in providing what you need, whether relationally or physically or emotionally—hear God's Word to you again and let it give you strength and security.

*"You will drink of the brook."*

If only you will look to your Father, remember His promises, and live in light of their assurances, you will not die from thirst while you're waiting with God in Cherith. Despite the disappointment, frustration, and real concern you may be feeling, "Don't worry about anything; instead, pray about everything" (Phil. 4:6, NLT). Because when He alone is your source, you can rest and be at ease despite the drying brook before you, behind you, or beside you. Your inner life can be nourished, pulsing with a peace that blossoms from His promises.

"My ultimate source of provision is God Himself."

**#ELIJAHBIBLESTUDY**

# Somewhere in Between

---

*"If they had been thinking of that country which they left, they would have had opportunity to return. But as it is, they desire a better country."*

**HEBREWS 11:15-16**

---

Joshua, my friend Shawna's older son, is a cadet at West Point, the United States Military Academy. West Point has made him different. Being a young Army cadet has shaved off whatever remained of any recklessness and frivolity, replacing it with self-discipline, respect and submission to authority, and honor for himself and for others around him.

It started in boot camp. First-year cadets—*plebes*, as the upperclassmen (not so lovingly) call them—arrive on campus with few freedoms. The rigid routine of their all-day, all-night schedule is harsh and unforgiving. Every single area of their lives is regulated. Unlike freshmen in other colleges, who can trot home every weekend for mama's cooking and laundry services, the rules regarding *plebes* restrict their family visits to a total of eight specific days for the entire two semesters, none of which exceed a strict 24–48 hours in duration.

That's just the military way. In order to be instilled with the mindsets, attitudes, priorities, and behaviors that will make them ready to discharge their duties in any situation, they need a clean, intentional distance from the life they were accustomed to living before entering the academy.

They need to resist the urge to go home.

> *Turn to and read Exodus 15:27-16:15. You're catching the children of Israel after they'd been delivered from Egypt, after they'd been chased by Pharaoh's army, and after they'd escaped through the Red Sea. Write the name of the place in verse 27 that tells us where they'd reached. What was it like?*

*According to Exodus 16:1, what was their location? This place was "between" Elim and where?*

*How does verse 2 describe this in-between place? How did the Israelites feel about being there? What did they do "against Moses and Aaron"?*

*In verse 3, how would you paraphrase the people's complaint about their current situation?*

They wished they were back home, even if home to them was altogether incompatible with the plan and purpose God had claimed on their lives. Or they wished they were going forward. And going there faster. They wanted to hurry on to Sinai where Moses said he'd met with God face to face, where the Lord had said to him, "When you have brought the people out of Egypt, you shall worship God at this mountain" (Ex. 3:12).

But from the middle of a dry, barren wilderness, all they could seem to think about were the dinner plates and aromas from the only home they'd ever known. They thought of it even more strongly than the prospect of being up-close and personal with God or of moving on from there to the "land flowing with milk and honey" that they'd been told was in their future (Ex. 13:5b).

They'd rather go back than go forward or rather go forward than just sit. The worst place of all, they believed, was being stuck there in-*between*.

*Now let's look again at our main passage, 1 Kings 17:2-5. I realize we've been in this passage for an extended stay, but I love studying the Bible this way, don't you? Bit by bit, line by line. Looking again at verse 3, what was the repeated geographical emphasis that was part of God's instructions to Elijah? In which direction did Yahweh want him to head?*

*Now flip to the map located at the back of your book.*

*• First, circle Samaria. This is where Elijah met with Ahab in verse 1, where he was currently located.*

*• Second, circle Tishbe. This, you'll recall, is where Elijah was born and raised.*

*• Third, find the Jordan River. God had told him to go just east of there to Cherith.*

*Consider the geographical position of these locations. How would you summarize Elijah's positioning and his potential dilemma?*

Elijah had been dead set on going to the palace, based on what his prophetic ears had picked up as God's immediate instructions concerning Ahab, Israel, and the coming drought. Yahweh's calling on his life had brought him out of his element and away from the comforts and familiarity of his home, down from the mountain passes and onto the road that led toward Samaria, capital city of the Northern Kingdom. Here is where he delivered his one-sentence, long-range forecast to the nation's ruler, making everyone uncomfortable, agitating Samaria's inhabitants with his prophetic declaration.

Then God told him to go back. Back east, toward home. But not to it.

Cherith was the in-between.

*When was the last time you longed impatiently to go home or to go back to the comfort and familiarity of a previous season of life that God clearly called you away from?*

*What are the easy-feeling, easygoing allures of "home" that most frequently tempt you away from the places and expectations that God's Spirit is leading you to press into?*

The comfort zone of home life can often be just as damaging to our spiritual growth as the enticing attraction of future ambition. That's why sometimes, in order to get us adequately prepared for the moments to come, God may not allow us to return to the way things used to be, the place where we could easily become lulled into complacency. When God needs us bold and fervent and clear of mind, He'll often call us to an in-between place. Not quite where we're going to be, but not all the way back where we were.

Elijah's wadi was in between Samaria and Gilead. Not quite there, not quite here. Neither the center of the action, nor the sweet spot of the sofa.

In order to prepare for Carmel, God sent Elijah not as far east as Elijah might have preferred to go. But if he hadn't listened and obeyed his Lord, if he'd scurried on home anyway, its comforts could have fostered complacency. And complacency could have robbed him of the character required for Carmel. He wouldn't have had the confidence in God, the trust in God's provision, that he learned by experience at the shallow, inadequate, in-between brook called Cherith.

The inadequacy of your Cherith is fortifying a holy courage and confidence you'll need for later. Don't shortcut the process. Life in the middle can be unsettling, but don't be discouraged. Stay put. Trust God, and in due time He'll move you on.

"Sometimes, in order to get us adequately prepared for the moments to come, God may not allow us to return to the way things used to be, the place where we could easily become lulled into complacency."

**#ELIJAHBIBLESTUDY**

## DAY FOUR
# Surprise, Surprise

---

*"I have commanded the ravens to provide food for you there."*

### 1 KINGS 17:4b

---

One of my favorite portions of Scripture is found at the end of the third chapter of Ephesians. The apostle Paul concluded the first half of his letter to the church at Ephesus with two verses that form one of the most spectacular doxologies in the whole New Testament.

> "Now to Him who is able to do exceedingly abundantly above all that we ask or think, according to the power that works in us, to Him be glory in the church by Christ Jesus to all generations, forever and ever. Amen."

**EPHESIANS 3:20-21, NKJV**

*Breathtaking, isn't it? Read those two verses again, and circle any words or phrases that resonate the most with you right now in your life.*

The part of Paul's praise song that makes my heart bubble with holy, excited anticipation is not only that God is able to accomplish things beyond my capacity to verbalize them in prayer (beyond what I can "ask"), but also that He can craft solutions and remedies for me beyond my ability to reason.

Beyond what I can THINK!

If you and I were blessed with the brightest minds in the world, we'd still remain limited in our thoughts about God, whether about His glory or His miraculous potential. We still wouldn't be in the same galaxy of comprehension where our omniscient, omnipresent, sovereign God operates every single day. Even when we're functioning at the highest levels of our cognitive capacities, we haven't yet reached the mere fringes of what is possible for Him to do.

In other words, your loving Father has categories of answers, solutions, and options for you and your life that you don't even know exist.

"Your loving Father has categories of answers, solutions, and options that you don't even know exist."

**#ELIJAHBIBLESTUDY**

They're beyond what you can think. Which, in part, is why God brought Elijah (and why His Spirit brings us) to Cherith—to show us things He can do that we would've never thought possible.

To surprise us.

Think of it. God not only intended to meet Elijah's need for water ("you will drink of the brook") but also for food—promises that were miraculous in themselves, given the isolated location of Cherith and the impending drought.

Elijah knew what the geography and environs around Cherith were like. This was dry, parched, thirsty, fallow ground. Even if he'd tried, Elijah knew he couldn't feed himself there. It was *unthinkable*.

God had put him in a position where no other options were possible—no other options than God Himself. Elijah had no choice but to trust God and God alone for His daily bread.

This is where the element of surprise showed up at Elijah's Cherith: "The ravens brought him bread and meat in the morning and bread and meat in the evening" (1 Kings 17:6).

*Ravens?!* Let's explore this together.

> **Centuries earlier, as Noah's ark floated across the flooded landscape of Earth, he sent out a raven, and later a series of doves, in search of dry land. Read a portion of this account in Genesis 8:6-9. Compare the behaviors of the two birds. What did the raven do that the dove didn't?**

> **What clues does this story give you about the normal tendency of ravens?**

> **Why might God have chosen a bird with this kind of inclination to bring meat and bread to Elijah each day?**

People who study such things say ravens rarely if ever return to the same place day after day. They're more famously known for their voracious appetite and insatiable greed. One author describes them as "flying garbage disposals"[3]—indiscriminate eaters who'll consume anything available.

Scholars believe Elijah may have been at Cherith for up to eighteen months.[4] If that's true, these ravens—these flocks of unsettled, unsharing, untrustworthy ravens—fed him roughly a thousand meals. I ask you: What were the odds of any bread and meat actually making it from the beaks of any kind of bird, much less this kind, to the breakfast and dinner table of Elijah in Cherith?

Perhaps if God had chosen doves or robins to perform this twice-daily, turn-down service, some kind of brilliant, brainiac bird expert could come up with a scientific hypothesis, describing how birds of that type might be capable of pinpointing a singular location day after day. God, however, chose a bunch of ravens for the job, thereby dispelling all rational theories.

It's just beyond what anyone would think. Or rationalize. Or could ever completely comprehend.

> **Look back over your life and recall a time when God sustained you in a way that was particularly shocking. Jot down a few details that defied reason and resisted rationalization. Prepare to share this story with your group when you meet again. Your testimony will build the faith of another sister.**

Cherith is designed to give us a front row seat to the unexplainable options of God, causing us to marvel sometimes not only at what He provides but how. Our experiences there translate into testimonies we tell to younger sisters coming up behind us, times when God used the most unreasonable person, or opened the most inconceivable door, or presented the most shocking opportunity or alternative or remedy in meeting our need. It never crossed our mind to pray that way. We hadn't even thought of it. But that's how God did it.

He did it like that!

Cherith teaches us to always leave God room for the element of surprise. He knows how to work through the most unlikely of delivery systems.

> *Consider a further reason why Elijah would never have thought of ravens as being an instrument God might use to care for him. Read the excerpt from Leviticus 11 (this is God talking to the early children of Israel), then record the insights you glean from it.*

> "You are to abhor these birds. They must not be eaten because they are abhorrent: eagles, bearded vultures, Egyptian vultures, kites, any kind of falcon, *every kind of raven*, ostriches, short-eared owls, gulls, any kind of hawk …"

**LEVITICUS 11:13-16, CSB, EMPHASIS MINE**

> *Given the historical relationship between ravens and Jews, what might your reaction have been if you were Elijah and God told you how He intended to deliver your miraculous meals?*

Elijah would've been taught the dietary principles of Leviticus 11 from a young age. If his mother ever caught him with a fried raven sandwich in his lunchbox, he'd have wished he hadn't traded for it. As a careful, law-abiding Jew, he would never have wanted to eat or touch anything associated with "abhorrent" ravens. These birds were culturally, religiously unclean. Repulsive.

And yet they were God's choice for feeding Elijah? Pretty unthinkable, if you ask me.

God will provide for you as His child, yes. But He's going to do more. He's going to surprise you. And it's going to grow your faith in the process.

> *Spend time in closing today with your heavenly Father, confessing any areas of resistance you feel toward His chosen ways of operating. And as you sit there, pouring out your heart to Him in honesty, surrender yourself to the freedom of receiving not only what He knows you really need, but also how He knows you really need it to arrive. Then ask Him to expose any areas of your life where pride or presumption needs to be replaced by humility and the tenderness of His Spirit.*

## DAY FIVE
# Shields Up

---

*"You are my hiding place; You keep me from trouble; You surround me with songs of deliverance."*

**PSALM 32:7**

---

Looking in retrospect, through the gift of hindsight, we see that while God was *sequestering* Elijah and *sustaining* him, even *surprising* him, He was also doing something else. He was *shielding* him from dangers that Elijah didn't realize were out there. God was shielding him from challenges Elijah wasn't yet prepared to handle.

**I've asked you before to think back, to see how God brought beauty and benefits from times in your life that seemed completely incapable of it. Today I'm asking it another way: How have you looked back on those times and discovered that God, by taking you through them when He did, was actually protecting you—keeping you safe from something or someone—shielding you from a possible outcome you didn't even know to be guarding against?**

**Let's fast-forward in Elijah's story, three years after he pronounced the judgment of famine on the land. Turn to 1 Kings 18:1-10. What did Elijah discover had been happening in Israel while he'd been hidden away at Cherith?**

*"As the LORD your God lives, there is no nation or kingdom where my master [Ahab] has not sent to search for you; and when they said, 'He is not here,' he made the kingdom or nation swear that they could not find you."*

**1 KINGS 18:10**

Yes, while Elijah had been tucked away by the drying wadi, many others knew what Elijah was just finding out. God had been strategically, intentionally shielding him from the searchlight of an angry king. Behind the biblical scenes, as we learn in 1 Kings 18, Ahab had been so outraged by Elijah's prediction that he'd sent a task force all over the land of Israel looking for this man he would later dub the "cause of disaster to Israel" (1 Kings 18:17). Ahab believed Elijah was at fault for all the difficulty this drought was causing, and he wanted the prophet to pay.

We have no indication Elijah was aware of any of this. Turns out Cherith—dull, drought-stricken Cherith—was actually God's secure hiding place that kept Elijah off the grid, out of radar range, where nobody would think to look for him no matter how intently they searched. Right there in the center of God's will, the prophet was supernaturally shielded so that any searchlights pointed in his direction were incapable of exposing his presence no matter how brightly they shone.

*Why is it so critical that we trust God with each season of life, resisting the urge to leave Cherith prematurely out of boredom, fear, or insecurity?*

I often have conversations with younger women who are carrying a number of goals and ambitions around with them. And they're discouraged. In their opinion, God has tucked them away on the rough, solitary, mundane soil of some "Cherith," and He's left them feeling forgotten and unfruitful. Their lives just aren't blossoming in the way they'd envisioned. Know the feeling?

This portion of Elijah's story that you and I are studying today is the one I often use to encourage them. In fact, my own experience is a case in point on this very theme.

Twenty years down the road now in ministry, I've seen how these Cherith seasons of my own—times when I felt the most unseen and unnoticed—were not only God's way of developing depths of spiritual maturity in me that I didn't yet possess. He was also shielding me from certain people, from certain opportunities, from certain outside influences, as well as from certain traps of the enemy that I had no idea awaited me. Not until much later did the Lord graciously allow me to see that the shadow I'd felt so discouraged inside was actually a holy shield keeping me out of view and under cover.

And you know what hindsight tells me?

It tells me I should've been grateful, not griping, in the middle of it.

Let's watch this same scenario play out in another portion of the Old Testament.

*Turn in your Bible to Exodus 13:17-18, which recounts God's dealings with ancient Israel, immediately after He miraculously freed them from four hundred years of slavery in Egypt.*

- How is the proximity of the "land of the Philistines" described?

- What was the Lord's concern in sending His people on this quicker, more convenient route? What was He *shielding* them from?

- What significant landmark would they encounter on the road He'd chosen for them?

- What miraculous experience would they have missed had He taken them on the path that was easier and more efficient?

The journey from Egypt to Canaan, if the children of Israel had been able to take the direct route, would've taken them roughly eleven days to complete. Just *eleven days!* Instead, God intentionally sent them on an indirect, much more inconvenient, much more time-consuming route. Why?

## 1. HE WAS PROTECTING THEM.

He was protecting them against the heavily armed forces of the Philistines. God's people were not yet organized well enough to defend themselves successfully against a far superior, far more battle-tested enemy. Furthermore, He was protecting them from themselves. Were they to walk into the teeth of the Philistines, God knew their next step would be a hasty retreat back toward captivity in Egypt. Better the enemy that you know than the one you've never seen and learned how to deal with.

## 2. HE WAS PUTTING THEM IN POSITION TO SEE HIS POWER.

Geographically, the Red Sea wasn't on the easy route. It was on the less traveled road, the itinerary that took them out of the way. Had He not hidden them along the highway where most people wouldn't expect them to travel, this particular miracle would never have happened and made it into the history books.

God was *shielding* them from danger. God was *shocking* them with what He could do.

> **In your own life right now, where do you feel as though God has chosen a longer, more inconvenient route for you to travel—in your school, your church, your extracurricular activities, or some other area that comes to mind?**

What has your reaction to it most regularly looked like?
- ○ Impatience?
- ○ Surrender?
- ○ Anger?
- ○ Gratitude?
- ○ Expectation?
- ○ Something else? _____

Maybe, just maybe, many years from now, you'll be digging through a box of old books and stuff, and you'll come across this Bible study. If that happens—and, oh, I hope it does—you'll come across this lesson that we're working through right now. You'll relive again the kinds of difficulties you've written about, the things you've been going through where perhaps you're questioning what God is doing.

In hindsight, you'll see that His grace and goodness have been with you all along. Even with everything you've endured and the difficulties you've faced, you'll see the faint outline of His holy shield that was keeping you guarded, protected, and secured. And you'll be able to whisper a heartfelt praise that may feel impossible for you to articulate right now. You'll see that He is good and His plans for you have always and only been good.

Even here. Under the shadows. At Cherith.

> "I remain confident of this: I will see the goodness of the LORD in the land of the living. Wait for the LORD; be strong and take heart and wait for the LORD."
>
> **PSALM 27:13-14, NIV**

# Zarephath

## THE SEASON OF REFINING

**Faith:** Committing to God's Process

# Dealing with Deficiency

*This week we are going with Elijah into uncharted territory. It's going to be an unfamiliar place for him and in many ways it is going to be uncomfortable.*

*And yet, he is going to be willing to go.*

*I know that if God allows our stories to intersect with Elijah's somehow then He is preparing us for the uncharted territories of faith that He wants to take us into. These could be unprecedented places that our families and friends have never walked into or new attitudes, dreams, and passions that He wants to cultivate in us.*

*As we launch into this week together, I felt compelled more than anything to pray over you. I want to pray in advance that before the Lord even calls you to wherever He wants to take you that you will already have the courage of the Holy Spirit to say yes to Him knowing He will equip and empower you there.*

Lord Jesus, I pray for my sister reading this right now.

I pray that You will ready her by Your Spirit. I pray that You will soften her heart so that she is sensitive to the whispers of Your sweet Holy Spirit, and that wherever You ask her to go and wherever You send her, she will unapologetically say yes.

Will You give her the courage to walk in the fullness of the abundant life in which You have called her?

In Jesus' name. Amen.

# Press Play

Here in Zarephath, Elijah is going to be _____. He's going to be _____. He's going to be _____ for Mount Carmel.

Faith is trusting God to go to an _____, unfamiliar place, and interact with people that it's unusual to interact with, so that God can use us to help inaugurate his move in _____ lives and _____ lives.

Elijah could have never known that by yielding to the unfamiliar, _____ territory where Yahweh sent him that he was actually helping to tell the entire _____ story.

# Discuss

**Read 1 Kings 17:8-12. Based on these verses, how would you describe the character of the widow?**

**What were Elijah's requests to the widow? Why does that seem like a ridiculous request?**

The first thing I noticed about her in verse 12 is that she says clearly, plainly, and honestly, "I have no food, only a handful of flour in the bowl and a little oil in the jar" (1 Kings 17:12). I love this about her. She is honest. She doesn't sugar coat her reality. She is authentic about her limitations.

She is honest about her lack and she dismantles any veneer of perceived perfection. She is forthcoming about what she has available. She brings it out in the open for Elijah who represents the presence of God. She brings it out in the open for him to deal with and to realize that this is not a cover-up. This is no time for self preservation. This is the time for authenticity.

> *What areas of your life do you feel like you lack when it comes to obeying God?*

> *Why do you tend to not be honest with the Lord about where you are?*

> *How can we promote authenticity with God and with other believers?*

I'm discovering in my walk with the Lord that sometimes authenticity is the hinge upon which a miracle rests. He's just waiting for me to be honest, because the reality is He knows anyway. Even if I'm not going to verbalize it, even if I'm not going to really share the actual real deal and be vulnerable, He knows. The widow teaches us to take an authentic inventory. Just go ahead and be real and honest with God.

But, let me also provide this warning. If we aren't careful, too much time on self-reflection and looking intrinsically can actually be to our detriment. And maybe that is why Elijah needed to give the widow a spur in the right direction for the next steps.

> *Read verse 13. What does Elijah say to the widow?*

When you're dealing with deficiency, yes, take an authentic inventory, but do not fear the miracle that God intends to do to you, for you, and then through you to somebody else. In this case, the widow's son was counting on her. It's going to require steps of faith. That fear will paralyze you from taking. Without a doubt, getting too wrapped up in your own inventory will drive you to a place of paralysis where you will assume that nothing can be done with the little bit that you have.

*How can fear keep us from walking in obedience?*

*More than 300 times in the Scripture we are told, "Do not fear" or "fear not."*

*What are practical ways we can fight against that fear?*

"For God gave us a spirit not of fear but of power and love and self-control."

**2 TIMOTHY 1:7, ESV**

# Press Play

Maybe you're at the stage where your faith needs to get a _____—it needs to go to _____.

Do what you _____ you would.

Those sticks you're gathering are not useless. They're the _____ for the _____ that God fully intends to set in your life.

# Discuss

**Why is it often difficult to put action behind our faith?**

**Read James 2:14-18. How does action reveal the authenticity of someone's faith?**

**Is there any area in your life where you're delaying obedience? What will it take for you to obey today?**

# DAY ONE
# Unsettled

*"Moab has been left quiet since his youth, settled like wine on its dregs. He hasn't been poured from one container to another or gone into exile. So his taste has remained the same, and his aroma hasn't changed."*

**JEREMIAH 48:11, CSB**

Comfort and steadiness are what we crave, but overstaying our welcome in one place can rob us of the work that God intends to do in us at the next one. In His wise and sovereign way, He often includes seasons of unsettledness where He transfers us out of the comfort and complacency of familiarity and moves us into a new place and position. It's a necessary part of His process.

**Looking back, what have been some of the most dramatic ways that you've experienced an "unsettling"?**

Each phase represents another refining stage in a divine progression of life. He deposits us into one season, with its own unique set of joys, challenges, people, and problems, and He lets us sit there a while. Pressing us. Sifting us. Purifying us. Then at the right time, when the work that needs to happen there is done, He unsettles us—sometimes in a way that feels forcible, sudden, and painful; other times in a nearly undetectable way that is organic, seamless, and can only be pinpointed in hindsight.

Either way, He strategically pours us into a new place and space—with new people, with new circumstances, with new life dynamics—knowing this new environment will be the most suitable for whatever He wants to reshape in us next.

Then He does it again and again—from a heart of love—for as long as we have breath in our lungs. He does it with our best interests in mind. He does it to make us better prepared for the Mount Carmels yet to come. Because if we're never "poured from one container to another," as Jeremiah 48:11 says, we stay unchanged. A foul taste remains in us. A foul aroma sticks to us.

*Open your Bible to 1 Kings 17:7-9. After reading these verses, meet me back here to answer the following questions:*

*Verse 7. How did Yahweh "unsettle" Elijah at Cherith? What did He allow to happen there?*

*Verse 8. What did God do in order to solidify to Elijah that he was supposed to move on?*

*Verse 9. Where's the next place that God poured Elijah into?*

By the time we come to verses 7-9, Yahweh was ready to pour Elijah into a new place around new people so that the process of refining could continue. But here's the clear yet difficult task for all of us who want to grow with God, glean the lessons He wants to teach, and move toward fulfilling our unique, divinely mandated purpose. We must IDENTIFY times of divine unsettling so we can release our grasp on one season and willingly move forward to the next, keeping our eyes, ears, and hearts open to receive everything God intends for us there.

For Elijah, and often for us, we can begin to identify a shift by recognizing the following two indicators:

## 1. THE DRYING BROOK

Elijah wasn't blind. He watched the brook of Cherith slowly dry up before his eyes. He knew his chances of survival in that secluded spot were going down, until finally the drought had baked his little creek bed into a bone dry ribbon of dust.

> *"It happened after a while that the brook dried up, because there was no rain in the land."*
>
> **1 KINGS 17:7**

Sometimes we can begin to discern that God is preparing to unsettle us when the resources needed to sustain us in our current position start to shrivel and dry up. And when these resources start to diminish, we must look to God. Every day. Don't let panic set in as you sit beside the drying brook. Instead, "cast your burden upon the LORD and He will sustain you" (Ps. 55:22). As you pray, God will either replenish your supply where you are or, as in Elijah's case,

He will keep on letting your brook dry up for the purpose of unsettling you and moving you onward.

> *Consider this in light of current circumstances in your life. Is there any way you've noticed your resources shrinking (emotional, physical, relational, financial, etc.)? What has your response been?*

If we aren't spiritually discerning, we'll be filled with alarm when our current resources begin drying up. We'll panic instead of trust, become filled with hopelessness instead of eager anticipation about what's to come. But Elijah's narrative helps us see the possibility that when finances fade, when opportunities dwindle, when skills and creativity decline, or when any number of necessities become increasingly unavailable, a new location could likely be awaiting our arrival.

So seek God like Elijah did. Tune your spiritual ears to hear what He might be cuing you toward. And then—listen to me closely now, because here's the part that goes against all our natural reflexes.

Let the brook go dry.

Don't scratch and claw to hang on to the droplets that remain. Rest. Trust. Don't be discouraged. He is unsettling you in order to prepare you, to push you, to move you to the next stage of your journey toward purpose.

## 2. THE CALL OF GOD

> *Look up the following verses before contemplating each question.*

| VERSES | |
|---|---|
| 1 Kings 17:2;<br>1 Kings 17:9;<br>1 Kings 18:1 | These verses possess a clear similarity. What is it? |

| 1 Kings 17:5;<br>1 Kings 17:10;<br>1 Kings 18:2 | These verses reveal Elijah's response to each one, each time. How would you describe it? |
| --- | --- |
| | |

We're not told how long Elijah sat beside a dry brook before Yahweh spoke, but we do know at the appropriate time, the same God who'd spoken so clearly to His servant about going to Cherith in the first place now confirmed the next move. The rain had stopped, but God's Word hadn't. At the right time, "the word of the Lord came to him" (1 Kings 17:8).

Before you can determine if and *when* to move and where to go, wait for your loving Father's clarity. Seek Him in prayer, listening for the gravity of the Spirit's conviction in your soul as He illuminates His Word. Seek the counsel of wise mentors and spiritual leaders. Because at the right time, He'll begin to shine a spotlight on the path He's planned for you to take toward Zarephath.

> **As we prepare to close our devotions today, stop right now and talk to the Lord. Confess any anxiety or panic you may feel in your situation. Ask Him to cause His peace to swell in your heart so you can patiently wait on His direction with confidence and patience. Use the space below to write your prayer.**

As the brook dried, Elijah realized what you and I need to realize. His heightened need was not so much a *problem* as an *opportunity* to hear afresh from God and launch out into a new direction. The prophet didn't manufacture his own plans for relief or wallow in his fears about the future. Instead, he trusted that God would speak just as He'd always spoken, giving him clarity on the next step. He believed the One who'd first called him out of Gilead, and then had given him clear direction to go to Cherith, would continue to be faithful. Elijah wasn't going anywhere until God made clear his next destination. And as soon as he got his orders, he knew what he would do. *Follow them.*

Straight to Zarephath.

# DAY TWO
# Anywhere but Here

*"Arise, go to Zarephath, which belongs to Sidon,
and stay there."*

**1 KINGS 17:9a**

The last couple of years for my extended family have been filled with one difficult circumstance after another. We have really walked through the fire. In fairly quick succession, a number of our close, beloved family members were taken from us by death—eight of them actually, each one hard in its own tragic way. My own sweet mother became diagnosed with a rare form of cancer, for which the doctors could offer few possible remedies. Within a matter of months, she was taken from our presence. Eight months later, my beloved mother-in-law unexpectedly and suddenly passed away. They're safe at home now with Jesus, but I miss them so much.

One week after my mother's funeral, in a visit to my own doctors, medical tests confirmed what they suspected and had been telling me. A nodule in my lung, which we'd been keeping our eye on for a while, had grown to an alarming size and would need to be taken out immediately. The invasive surgical procedure to remove the entire upper lobe of my left lung revealed what we were afraid to discover: the nodule was cancerous. Gratefully, the surgery was curative—they were able to get it all—but the recovery and rehabilitation were grueling.

I don't know the details of your personal story, but I do know what all of us went through in the days following my surgery: COVID-19, the global pandemic; followed by the death of an African-American man in police custody, sparking unmitigated racial tensions that flared up into large-scale protests, isolated incidents of rioting, and volatile unrest across America. I'm just saying: whatever amount of life you've experienced, you've been through seasons marked by the fires of hardship and trial. I'm sure of it. Times when you've wanted to be anyplace else.

*Anywhere but here.*

Elijah felt somewhat the same way—about Zarephath.

**Notice the definition of *Zarephath* in the margin. How does this single piece of information parallel with what we've already learned about the way God matures and grows His children?**

*The name* **ZAREPHATH** *comes from a word that means "smelting furnace" or "refining."*[1]

Elijah would've felt the same way about his "anywhere but here" location that we often feel about ours: *uncomfortable*. The sanctifying work of fire always is. But that's what Zarephath was for Elijah—an introduction to a further season of refining. This location was an unlikely and unusual destination for Yahweh to send Elijah for several reasons.

The first, more general reason is that it was a small village located outside of Israel (did you notice that on the map?) in a population center known for being steeped in pagan idolatry. The primary citizens of Zarephath were *Baal worshipers* through and through, whose reverence for their fake deity inflamed them into flagrant, unrestrained acts of religious (should I say, irreligious) fervor.

The second, more specific reason is this: Ethbaal had a daughter named *Jezebel*. And this region of Sidon was her home. Here she'd been reared into the woman who nearly singlehandedly introduced the unhindered worship of Baal among God's people. Once she became the wife of Israel's King Ahab, she used her evil, bullheaded influence to foist Baal worship on the entire nation. She would later hunt down Elijah with designs to kill him for daring to champion the cause of monotheistic worship to the one true God, the worship of Yahweh.

And, yes, that's where God was sending him—to the place where Elijah's chief enemy had been raised.

But wait, I'm getting ahead of myself. Let's stop here and look around Zarephath for a minute, the way it existed at this moment in Elijah's personal life, before Mount Carmel ever came into the picture. Try to think of it as if you were seeing it for the first time through the prophet's own horrified eyes.

*Think how this location would make a Jewish man like Elijah, who absolutely despised idolatry, feel uncomfortable. What kinds of emotional or mental hurdles would Elijah need to push past in order to obey God by going to Zarephath, both in action and in attitude?*

*In what ways do you think Elijah could be refined and purified by going to Zarephath despite its unique dynamics?*

For this next question, you'll need to revisit 1 Kings 17:9. How did God tell Elijah to treat his time in Zarephath?

○ Visit there
○ Stay there
○ Pass through it
○ Prophecy against it

*Think of a place or position where God has set you right now that, for whatever reason, bristles against your comfort. How does this uncomfortable dynamic reshape your perspectives, refine your behaviors, and reframe your attitudes? Be as specific as you can.*

*Answering honestly, being neither too hard nor too easy on yourself, how would you describe your response to this unwanted place you're staying in? (Mark any that apply.)*

○ Constantly on edge, longing for it to change
○ Still hopeful, despite the difficulty of it
○ Discouraged and, frankly, discontent
○ Surrendered to this season of life
○ Watching for God's hand in it

As I've said before, we can either *resist* or *surrender* to divine disruptions, both in attitude and in action. The Lord leaves us those options. We can either refuse to listen, doubt His sovereignty, fester with bitterness, and miss learning the lessons He wants to teach us in this new location—OR—we can "stay there," lean in, and directly engage this place where He's taken us, despite our discomfort, submitting ourselves to the fire in which we will be refined.

So right here, right now, I want to revisit the question that you and I dealt with on our first day together in this study, when we agreed with each other about how badly we all want the faith and fire of Elijah in our lives. Remember what we asked ourselves?

### ARE WE WILLING TO DO WHAT ELIJAH DID TO GET WHAT ELIJAH GOT?

*Knowing now that Zarephath may put you in the line of "fire," what's your sincere answer to this question today? (Answer honestly. God hears. He sees. And His grace is sufficient for us.)*

> "We can either resist or surrender to divine disruptions, both in attitude and in action."
>
> **#ELIJAHBIBLESTUDY**

Zarephath felt too hot to touch. Elijah couldn't possibly have wanted it any more than he'd wanted Cherith. But think what the Lord was preparing to forge in him from within this furnace: godly maturity, relational wisdom, depth of character, compassion for others, courage in the face of adversity, spiritual openness and preparedness. And since nothing of value in God's kingdom is ever achieved quickly or without cost, this stop on Elijah's journey was going to be worth it. For him and for us.

When you find yourself in a season of trial, believe that God in His sovereignty has brought you here. He is directing you here "so that the proof of your faith, being more precious than gold which perishes though tested by fire, may be found to result in praise, glory, and honor at the revelation of Jesus Christ" (1 Pet. 1:7). This place matters. This fire is for refining.

Elijah was headed to Zarephath. There in that city, he would be purified by the circumstances he would face, by the people he would meet, and by the opportunities for divine encounters that he would discover.

And so will we.

# Anyone but Her

*"Behold, I have commanded a widow there*
*to provide food for you."*
**1 KINGS 17:9b**

Picture this: a hungry, exhausted, unkempt Jewish man sitting by the city gates of a pagan town. Signs of the ongoing drought that have been ravaging the entire region are visible in his face, in his ribs, in the gaunt, dusty condition of his appearance. A quick look around reveals that these same signs are not just his; they're everywhere—in the faces of everyone who passes by, in everyone who lives there.

What no one can tell, however, even if they notice him looking around, is that he's looking for someone he's never seen before. The only clue he's been given is that she's a widow, living here in Zarephath, and that she's somehow connected to his future in this town, for as long as God decides to keep him here. Other than that, he's operating on pure, prophetic instinct. He's simply trusting the Lord to point her out to him.

There, is that her? No? What about this one? No.

He sits. He scans. He knows she's out there somewhere.

Then finally, he sees her. He's sure of it. He supernaturally realizes that this lonely, lean woman gathering up broken sticks for kindling, her forehead etched with worry and concern, is the one he's been dispatched to find. This woman with the fatigued, desperate look on her face is the same person God has said will provide sustenance for Elijah in the midst of this drought.

*THIS woman, Lord? This hungry, helpless, Gentile woman?*

*Oh, dear God, anywhere but* here. *And anyone but* her.

The weakest, most vulnerable people on the socioeconomic ladder during Elijah's day were women. But the marginalization that every woman experienced, solely because of her gender, was heightened even further if the woman happened to be unmarried; even worse if she were widowed. A widow truly existed on the fringes of society.

So not only had God commanded Elijah to go to a *place* that seemed unreasonable, He'd also called him to make connections there with a *person* who was thought to be nothing. Insignificant. Of little to no value.

And to cap off the complete absurdity of this unsavory situation, God hadn't sent Elijah to Zarephath to be the strong man who would provide for *her*. The widow had been tapped by Yahweh to be the avenue of provision for *him*.

> **Is receiving assistance from others or causing them inconvenience difficult for you to accept? Why or why not?**

> **Could this be one of the places where you need the fire of refining? How so? Which pieces of this attitude need to be burned up and consumed?**

*A **WIDOW** had no identity, sense of belonging, or security. During this famine, she and her son would have been starving. The city gate was where people could possibly help her— the place where life change was possible for someone without a means to provide more for herself than the last bit of flour and oil she had left.*

In Cherith, Elijah had been on the receiving end of God's miraculous provision for maybe a year and a half. He was accustomed now to being in need, to feeling dependent, to knowing what it was like not having sufficient resources to care for himself.

And yet this new assignment in the furnace of Zarephath would've refined him in another unique way. Because it's one thing for a flock of birds to bring you meat and bread. No one else is there to witness you up-close at your worst and neediest. It doesn't require authenticity. You don't have to be real with ravens.

But you do have to be real with a widow when she's standing right there in front of you, when she's the one who's providing you room and board and can see your need at close range. At Zarephath, you graduate to a harder test. Zarephath requires vulnerability. Zarephath involves a baring of soul that can't be masked or covered with makeup. Zarephath leaves no space for being less than honest about what's harbored in your heart.

Zarephath cuts you down to size.

Not only would Elijah's pride, self-reliance, and any sense of supremacy be purified during his relationship with this person—this "anyone but her" person—but by submitting to Zarephath, Elijah was being positioned for things more impactful and far-reaching than he could ever have imagined.

### 1. A PARTICIPANT IN GOD'S BIGGER PLAN.

This encounter the Lord set in motion between Elijah and a Gentile widow pointed to much more than simply a famine survival strategy for one solitary man.

> *Read Galatians 3:26-28 in the margin, then answer this question: How did Elijah's interaction with a Gentile widow begin to reveal God's overarching story of redemption?*

*"For you are all sons and daughters of God through faith in Christ Jesus. For all of you who were baptized into Christ have clothed yourselves with Christ. There is neither Jew nor Greek, there is neither slave nor free, there is neither male nor female; for you are all one in Christ Jesus."*

**GALATIANS 3:26-28**

In Zarephath, God would testify that His ultimate plan for the redemption of humanity didn't extend to only one group of people but to everyone—the disenfranchised, marginalized, and forgotten. This encounter would begin to reveal His heart toward all people of all ages, in every demographic. Elijah's connection to the widow would model the fact that no one has a monopoly on God's grace, that His redemptive plan is much larger than one single nationality or class. It includes people from every tongue, tribe, nation, and station.

We know this concept now as the gospel, a spiritual reality that is far wider in vantage point than anything Elijah could have fathomed.

> *Turn to Acts 10:34-35. Reading these two verses, you'll hear the apostle Peter coming to terms with this same, inclusive message of the gospel. Where do you perhaps fall short, allowing prejudices that you've been taught or have picked up along the way to prevent you from being as open toward others as you ought to be?*

"No one has a monopoly on God's grace … His redemptive plan is much larger than one single nationality or class. It includes people from every tongue, tribe, nation, and station."

**#ELIJAHBIBLESTUDY**

Without even needing to understand what God was up to, Elijah's willingness to follow His lead—establishing a relationship with an "anyone but her" person—linked him into an experience that glorified God and is still speaking to us today.

> *How does this reminder about God's larger plan add perspective, even value, to the people the Lord has strategically placed in your path right now? How does it help you rest in God's sovereignty?*

## 2. A PARTNER IN GOD'S MIRACULOUS PROVISION.

Yes, it started with Elijah being meek and humble. It started with choosing to present himself empty—as empty as the widow woman he flagged down in the streets of Zarephath. Elijah's authenticity would be how God taught him that he wasn't so different from this Gentile widow after all. They both needed water; they both needed bread.

But emptiness, when acknowledged, is often what builds bridges to others. It intersects you with someone else's lack, where God can then use you as a catalyst for their own encounter with Him. By the time we reach tomorrow's lesson, bread and oil will miraculously start to multiply in the widow's house. From a place of needing to be fed himself, he will introduce others to the God who can feed them too. This is what Zarephath teaches us. Being honest about our own lack comes first, then we get the privilege of becoming a partner in God's miraculous provision.

Sister, maybe you thought the scarce, lacking, dried-up places in your life would turn out to be the reasons why God *couldn't* use you, why He *couldn't* do anything significant through you. But these points of marked emptiness are actually the keys that open doors of ministry for you and of God's miracles through you. It's where your deficiencies line up for you to intersect with destiny.

With *anyone but her.*

For Elijah, his own need is what built a bridge to the widow's need. And Yahweh used it as the basis of a miracle for both of them.

## DAY FOUR

# What I See, What He Says

---

*"We look not at the things which are seen, but
at the things which are not seen; for the things which are
seen are temporal, but the things
which are not seen are eternal."*

**2 CORINTHIANS 4:18**

---

These next few verses are too breathtaking and unforgettable not to be read in their entirety. I've printed them here for you. Linger in this passage and soak in every detail of God's power. Watch Him use Elijah, after seeing the widow gathering wood nearby, to provide hope and peace where there had been neither, to provide food and water where both had been in diminished supply. Most of all, watch Him care enough to introduce Himself to one woman— forgotten by others but known and seen by a loving Father.

> [10] Elijah called to her and said, "Please bring me a little water in a cup and let me drink." [11] As she went to get it, he called to her and said, "Please bring me a piece of bread in your hand."
>
> [12] But she said, "As the LORD your God lives, I don't have anything baked—only a handful of flour in the jar and a bit of oil in the jug. Just now, I am gathering a couple of sticks in order to go prepare it for myself and my son so we can eat it and die."
>
> [13] Then Elijah said to her, "Don't be afraid; go and do as you have said. But first make me a small loaf from it and bring it out to me. Afterward, you may make some for yourself and your son, [14] for this is what the LORD God of Israel says, 'The flour jar will not become empty and the oil jug will not run dry until the day the LORD sends rain on the surface of the land.'"

¹⁵ So she proceeded to do according to the word of Elijah. Then the woman, Elijah, and her household ate for many days. ¹⁶ The flour jar did not become empty, and the oil jug did not run dry, according to the word of the LORD he had spoken through Elijah.
**1 KINGS 17:10b-16, CSB**

See, wasn't that good? Now think through and respond to the following questions:

- What do the opening few words of verse 11 tell you about the widow's heart?

- How did she describe the status of her food supply in verse 12?

- What had she concluded about her and her son's future?

- What similar realities had Elijah faced at Cherith?

*Look back again at 1 Kings 17:14, where Elijah gave the widow hope amid her desperate condition. Write down the first clause from verse 14 below.*

*What do these words tell you about Elijah's perspective regarding the widow's circumstances?*

In the despair of the moment, this widow was consumed by what she could see. Elijah, however, reported what God had *said.*

### WHAT WE *SEE* / WHAT HE *SAYS*

Now put down your pen and just read the next few paragraphs with a prayerful perspective. This "what we *see* / what He *says*" of Elijah's statement pinpoints the hinge that separates hope from hopelessness, possibility from

"What God says pinpoints the hinge that separates hope from hopelessness, possibility from impossibility."

**#ELIJAHBIBLESTUDY**

impossibility. His statement "Thus says the LORD God of Israel" and the perspective it represents changed the entire trajectory of the widow's story.

Elijah's time in Cherith is what enabled his faith reflex to be so easily ignited during his interaction with the widow. He seemed almost to jump at the chance to introduce God's provision and promise to her. He didn't minimize her lack or pretend it wasn't real, but he also didn't rehearse it or stew on it. Instead he emphasized the *word of the Lord* that applied to her specific circumstance.

> *"He comforts us in all our affliction, so that we may be able to comfort those who are in any kind of affliction, through the comfort we ourselves receive from God."*
>
> **2 CORINTHIANS 1:4, CSB**

The same is true for you, my friend. Among the reasons for why God has placed you in that classroom, in your neighborhood, or in that organization, after having gone through the experiences that He's allowed into your life, is because they create a point of contact between the promises of God that you've hidden in your heart and the people around you who are hurting.

**Who do you know that needs to be reminded of the promises of God? Will you succumb to fear or will you help elevate them to God's truth?**

Impossibility is God's starting point. The people who live around you, even the ones who only infrequently pass in and out of your life—each of them needs to know that "with God all things are possible" (Matt. 19:26).

Part of your privilege as His child is to keep this limitless perspective and expectation continually before your eyes so that His Word is continually in your mouth, poised to deliver His encouragement to others.

Listen to me: Zarephath strategically brings you face to face with someone else's impossibility—the failed exam, the sick grandparent, the messy divorce, the crippling depression. Hear them and sincerely empathize when they tell you what they *see*, but don't leave the conversation without inserting what their omniscient, omnipresent, sovereign, promise-keeping God *says*.

If you don't, who will?

So, friend, here are the questions that today's whole lesson hinges upon: (1) Are you investing time into searching God's Word—discovering His heart,

His perspective, and His promises that apply to us today—so that you know what He has said about situations like these?

Or (2) are you caught up and swept away in the same vortex of hopelessness that the people in front of you are feeling, where you can only commiserate with them in their pain instead of speaking the truth in love and appropriately inserting God's vantage point into the conversation at every opportunity?

Take these questions and your heart responses to the Lord in prayer. Use the margin as journaling space for your honest thoughts. Ask Him to show you how He has called you to be an "Elijah"—a spokesperson for His promises—to every "widow" you come into contact with. Ask Him to make your commitment to His Word so strong that it not only governs your behavior, speech, and attitude, but also spills from your lips instinctively. Regularly. Naturally.

Zarephath's widows need a word from the Lord. And you, modern-day Elijah, need to know it so you can share it. This is Zarephath's challenge to you. To me. To us.

Hope hinges on it.

> As you wrap up today, here are just a few of the sweet, strong promises of God that you can use immediately to encourage others in their struggles and distresses. When you have time, look up several or all of these verses, being careful to consider the context around them. See if God may already be lining up one or more of them to speak *precisely* to a need that you're familiar with in someone else's life:
>
> - Deuteronomy 31:6
> - Joshua 1:9
> - Psalm 23:4
> - Proverbs 29:25
> - Isaiah 41:10
> - Lamentations 3:57
> - Daniel 10:12
> - Luke 12:7
> - John 14:27
> - Hebrews 13:6
> - 1 Peter 3:14
> - Revelation 2:10
>
> *Who can you call or text to share one of these assurances with, helping to calm their anxious hearts and stay anchored in truth?*

# Open in Prayer

---

*"The woman said to Elijah, 'Now I know that you are a man of God, and that the word of the LORD in your mouth is truth.'"*

**1 KINGS 17:24**

---

I want us to start today's study by reflecting on where you are in your personal prayer life. Here we go.

**On the scales below—with 1 being really uncomfortable; 10 being really natural—circle the numbers that correspond to your comfort level with:**

**Private prayer (alone with God)**

---

1    2    3    4    5    6    7    8    9    10

**Public prayer (in front of others)**

---

1    2    3    4    5    6    7    8    9    10

**Do you typically struggle more to ask God for things that seem small or the larger, supernatural, miraculous kind of requests? Why?**

Today's last lesson from Zarephath is about this all-important issue of prayer. That's because "after these things," the Bible says (1 Kings 17:17)—after God had been daily, miraculously providing meal service for Elijah and the widow— something terrible happened. Her son came down with a severe illness serious enough that he died from it. And in the wake of this tragedy, we're about to see an additional aspect of Elijah's spiritual life and character being refined and fortified for future use.

Think how unconscionable this stunning turn of events must have seemed to them. To both of them. They thought they'd dodged the famine bullet. God had been remarkably feeding them, enough for them to live on every single day, presumably *to keep them alive!* But now it all seemed for nothing. This mother's greatest fear had become her reality anyway.

And she immediately started assigning blame.

> **Turn to 1 Kings 17:18-20. Focusing for now on just verse 18, as the widow was hysterical with grief, paraphrase her outburst against Elijah.**

> When was the last time you were unjustly accused of something and what was your response to it?
> ○ Defended myself
> ○ Kept quiet
> ○ Passed blame off to another person
> ○ Something else _____

I am intrigued and challenged by Elijah's reaction to the widow's accusations. Instead of defending himself, instead of returning her emotional volley, instead of taking offense at her attack on his "man of God" reputation, he was mainly silent, calm, and compassionate. He didn't react in any of the ways I usually do when shade is thrown my direction. As proof that he'd absorbed well the lessons of Gilead, Cherith, and now Zarephath, he looked away from his accuser and upward to the Lord.

> "Then he cried out to the LORD and said, 'LORD my God, have you also brought tragedy on the widow I am staying with by killing her son?'"
>
> **1 KINGS 17:20, CSB**

Elijah immediately took his concerns into prayer.

As God matures and refines us, life's crises won't be as capable of flipping the switch inside us that rams us into fear and anxiety mode. Instead, they will trigger a natural reaction within us to call out, to cry out, to the Lord. To trust Him. To rely on His sovereignty. To reach out in faith, believing our God is "able to do exceedingly abundantly above all that we ask or think" (Eph. 3:20, NKJV). The lessons Elijah learned about prayer in Zarephath will teach him how to *call down fire* on Mount Carmel. Let's see if we can walk away with three lessons in prayer that Elijah's example teaches us.

> "He said to her, 'Give me your son.'"
>
> **1 KINGS 17:19a**

## 1. TAKE THE WHOLE PROBLEM TO GOD IN PRAYER.

When Elijah scooped up the widow's lifeless son, he was literally carrying the problem to the Lord. He was presenting to Him the entire, devastating reality that he'd just witnessed. There would be no masking the issue, no denial of what was happening, no sugarcoating of details to make the gravity of the scene any more palatable. This was no time for pious rituals or platitudes, but simply for going all-in with the only One who could infuse life-giving power into this situation.

*Is there a glaring need or battle in your life right now that you haven't fully presented to God in prayer? Take a moment to stop, pray, and repent of the pride that has kept you from releasing everything to God and then get real about it. Bring it on. Bring it all.*

## 2. CULTIVATE A PLACE OF PRIORITY IN PRAYER.

> "He took him from her arms, carried him to the upper room where he was staying, and laid him on his bed."
>
> **1 KINGS 17:19b, NIV**

Many scholars believe that this "upper room" where Elijah took the body of the dead child was likely the space in the house where he'd done a lot of praying already. He was accustomed to going there for the purpose of prayer. It was where he regularly met with God.

I'll be the first to say there's nothing magic about a specific place when it comes to praying. We can pray at school, pray in the kitchen, pray in our bedroom, pray in the backyard. But having a specific *place* of prayer can signify the *priority* we've placed on prayer. That's the point (See Matt. 6:6). Elijah knew exactly where to take that boy, straight up into the room where God had shown up so powerfully so many times.

*What might it look like for you to set aside a place where you can regularly run to God in prayer? What value could be gained from doing that?*

## 3. EXPECT GOD TO ANSWER UNREASONABLE PRAYERS.

> "He stretched himself out over the boy three times, and called to the LORD and said, 'LORD, my God, please, let this boy's life return to him.' And the LORD listened to the voice of Elijah, and the life of the boy returned to him and he revived."
>
> **1 KINGS 17:21-22**

There's not a single record from any earlier Scripture that hints at a precedent for a resurrection prayer. And there's certainly no prescription for his decision to lay himself across the boy's body. In fact, according to Jewish law, touching a human corpse resulted in a seven-day quarantine (see Num. 19:11). Ordinarily, Elijah would've considered this physical contact with a dead body as being exceptionally vile and unclean. And yet his compassion for this family, a compassion forged in the fire of his own need and suffering, trampled all protocols. He blazed his own trail, launching a prayer so bold into the heavens that no one else in recorded biblical history had ever employed it before.

Only one thing can account for this level of expectation and trust in the power of Almighty God. The journey through Gilead, Cherith, and Zarephath had turned spiritual concept into spiritual concrete. Elijah didn't just *have* faith anymore. Elijah *lived* faith.

His faith had caught fire.

*If you were to make an unreasonable, unthinkable prayer today, what do you think it would be? (You're not limited to one. Think of as many as you can.)*

*Then pray it. Do it right now. Let your faith be set ablaze.*

I almost hesitate to interrupt you. Ending this lesson on prayer, by being in prayer, is such a fitting way to transition from the first half of our study to the next. Praying at a new level of believing faith feels like the perfect way of capturing what God has been pouring into our lives throughout these three strong weeks. Thank you for hanging in with me this far.

This is what we want, isn't it? Whatever it takes to get here. We want faith that can believe God for moments like this one, when Elijah walked back into that widow's house, with her son walking right beside him. "Now I know that you are a man of God," she exclaimed, not knowing which one to hug the hardest. "The word of the LORD in your mouth is truth" (1 Kings 17:24).

Our lives can compel those closest to us to know our God reigns. Our faith can excite them to discover the power of God for themselves, even as we continue to grow and mature, developing strength and fortitude in the process. We're certainly going to need it.

Mount Carmel is coming.

# Carmel

## EXPOSING THE COUNTERFEIT

 **Fire:** Submitting to God's Power

# Don't Drop the Ball

*Welcome to the midpoint of our Bible study!*

*Listen, I know what can happen when you get to the middle of any serious project. One of two extremes can happen. For some, this is where you start feeling a little apathetic or indifferent. You look back and see all that you've accomplished, so you decide to just skim by until you get to the end. And for others on the opposite extreme, you may feel really motivated and just want to rush to get it finished as soon as you possibly can.*

*But I want to warn you against either extreme.*

*Instead, I want you to pause right here and I want you to guard yourself from rushing forward and just trying to finish. I also want you to make a commitment to not lose your motivation. I don't want you to miss out on experiencing what God might speak to you if you don't continue to dive into the pages ahead.*

*Just breathe.*

*Celebrate what you've already accomplished, then intentionally look forward to what it is that God wants to continue to do in your life. Remember that Bible studies like this one and all the time you spend in God's Word is never about finishing. It is about refining.*

*It's about the work of God that He intended to do in your life when you first started. It's about the purification in you. It's about how He is molding you into the image of Jesus. It's about how He's changing your perspectives and your mindsets in order to make you more and more like Him.*

*So as you move forward into this week and all that follows, take a deep breath and enjoy your time with the Lord.*

# Press Play

There's a _____ that sits right between Elijah's time at Zarephath and his coming experience on Mount Carmel, and this link, this bridge, is _____.

Obadiah was _____.

He was _____-_____.

He was _____ at his _____.

He was a _____ _____.

Building up _____ in heaven is not a pass for being useless or ineffective on _____.

# Discuss

Describe where God has placed you right now to be effective for His kingdom. What school, teams, organizations, or activities are you involved in?

How might God want to use you right where you're at?

Why do Christians sometimes coast through life with no regards for God's earthly kingdom?

I want to encourage you that wherever God has placed you, that's the position where he fully intends to work out His purpose for your life, right in the midst of wherever you find yourself right now. Stop downplaying the significance of your position. Stop undervaluing how critical and purposeful your current posture is.

You're necessary. Hear that again.

You are necessary, and you're necessarily right where you are.

It's by divine appointment that you are in that neighborhood. It's by divine appointment that you're in that classroom, or that you're on that public university campus as a counselor. It's by divine appointment that you are on that team, or that you're a part of that club. It is not accidental, it's strategic. You've been placed there for a reason.

> *How does knowing that God has purposefully placed you right where you are change the way you view your current place in life?*

Obadiah shows us that there's something to be said about having a strategic position, where you recognize God's hand is on you. Did you know that God's hand is on you even as a middle school or high school student? He's not just leading the missionaries or your pastors or your Sunday school and Bible study leaders. He's leading you. God's hand is on you right where He has placed you, to be used for His purposes and His glory.

Keep your spiritual eyes open, and don't drop the ball.

> *Read 1 Kings 18:3-5. How does verse 3 describe Obadiah's relationship with the Lord?*

> *What does Obadiah do in these verses that reveals his faith in the Lord is genuine?*

As some were actively destroying and seeking to obliterate the rule and authority of Yahweh, Obadiah was actively protecting and preserving it. There's something to be said, not only about a strategic position, but also about an unwavering pledge, and a fierce protection and preservation of the things of God. And so, in an antagonistic culture, he was not passive. He was not inactive in his mission to uphold the things of God. He was risking his very life.

## Press Play

*What are you _____ doing to make sure you are _____ the _____ of God in this generation?*

*Don't drop the _____ on your watch.*

*Just in doing your job, that _____ _____, leads to a moment of _____ _____.*

# *Discuss*

*How can you stand for truth and preserve God's Word in your generation?*

*When have you experienced God showing up in a divine way in the middle of something that felt ordinary or mundane?*

*Where do you need God to show up in a divine way in your life right now?*

# Rain and Fire

*"Now it happened after many days that the word
of the* Lord *came to Elijah in the third year, saying,
'Go, show yourself to Ahab, and I will provide rain on
the face of the earth.'"*

**1 KINGS 18:1**

Think back to the last time you had to wait for something, every day, for an extended period of time. An important text from a friend? An acceptance letter from a certain college? Word that you made the team? Remember how you felt—going to bed each night, then waking up each morning, hoping *surely* this would be the day you'd hear something. You didn't know if you could wait much longer.

Every day for three and a half years—roughly 1,277 days—the people of Israel had squinted into the sun-streaked skies wondering when in the world this drought would break. Scientists who study such things can measure the depleting effects of drought on crops, soil, and water supply after as little as *one week* of no rain, much less a year, two years, three years. What they can't measure, only observe, is the mental and emotional toll it takes—especially in an agricultural society like the Israel of Elijah's day—the daily stress of trying to wring out enough resources to care for your family, fields, and flocks, when your whole economy hinges on it.

It's why King Ahab, as I shared with you in this week's video session, had taken the extreme action of going out *himself* as part of a surveying team, along with his trusted (and God-fearing) advisor Obadiah, in desperate hopes of finding enough grass to keep the livestock alive.

Into this state of events and emotions—where *every day* they wished for rain—the "word of the Lord came to Elijah," declaring that He was calling an end to this divinely orchestrated attempt at getting His people's attention.

Yahweh was preparing to send down the rain.

*In this season of your life, is there something you've been fixated on—something you've desired in the same way the Israelites desired rain? Something relational? Financial? Material? School-related? Family-related? What is it?*

*What has the delay in receiving it given to you or produced in you? What has this unmet need/want presented?*

"Seasons of waiting—seasons of want—can be golden opportunities for growth, development, preparation, and refining."

**#ELIJAHBIBLESTUDY**

As we've learned from Elijah's life, seasons of waiting—seasons of want—can be golden opportunities for growth, development, preparation, and refining. When we surrender them to the Lord, when we receive them as an importantly patient, painful part of a useful sanctifying process, He causes them to produce things of great value in our lives. Faith. Resilience. Godly perspective. Deeper, more personal intimacy with Him. There is *purpose* in the deprivation.

*Turn to 1 Kings 18:17-18, which reports on the first face-to-face encounter between Ahab and Elijah in three years. In reading the words they shared, compare and contrast the perspective that each man possessed regarding this ordeal.*

• *Ahab (v. 17)*

• *Elijah (v. 18)*

*Now read the two verses from Isaiah 26 in the margin, and answer the following questions:*

• What are God's "judgments" designed to instill in people's hearts?

"When the earth experiences Your judgments, the inhabitants of the world learn righteousness. Though the wicked is shown compassion, he does not learn righteousness; he deals unjustly in the land of uprightness, and does not perceive the majesty of the LORD."

**ISAIAH 26:9B-10**

- *Consider the concept of "learn[ed] righteousness"? What does this mean, and what does it look like?*


- *How do you see Ahab's reaction mirrored in the three closing statements of verse 10?*


The revelation of God's majesty to a double-minded nation and its hard-hearted king was the primary objective of the consequences they had suffered. In other words, it wasn't really about the rain at all. The lack of water was just for context. The drought conditions were the result of Israel's failure to adhere to the covenant, yes, but they were simultaneously a catalyst designed to turn the heart of the nation back to Him and to highlight His deity.

So after three difficult years, the people and their king understandably thought their greatest need was for something to bathe in and cook in and grow their food in. But this was not Yahweh's most pressing desire for them. Their greatest need—always our greatest need—was for God Himself. Elijah knew this.

And now the people were about to know it too.

The prophet, having learned from Gilead, and from Cherith, and from Zarephath, and from the word of the Lord growing stronger and clearer and more vibrant in his heart at each step along the way, was ready now to press the issue. The time had come for Ahab and for Israel to climb up to the mountain and get a firsthand view of what they didn't even realize was their most pressing, primary need.

Before rain, fire!

*Now read 1 Kings 18:19, where Elijah declared the terms of his proposal, before there was to be any rain.*

Who was to come?
- All _____
- 400 prophets of _____
- 450 prophets of _____
- Those who were supported by _____

Where were they to assemble?
- Mount _____

After such a long time of dryness, everybody believed the end of the drought must finally be at hand. Their eyes were peeled to the heavens looking for rain. With this mass call and holy movement to the mountain, the conversations along the roads and trails leading up to Carmel must have buzzed with excited anticipation. The last time they'd heard from the prophet Elijah, he had called off the rain. Surely he'd returned now to call it back on. To slake their thirst. To raise his hands toward the heavens from the top of Mount Carmel and appeal to Yahweh for the clouds to open up once again. To give them what they *wanted*.

But the people were soon to see that they hadn't been called up here to get a desired taste of *water* from heaven but a needed blast of *fire* from heaven. They knew what they wanted, but God knew what they needed first—a fresh revelation and experience with Him—even above the thing that they perceived to be their greatest need at the moment.

Sometimes, in the moment of drought, we can often assume that our deepest physical desire is an accurate reflection of our truest need. But what *God* wants to give us—the Holy Spirit, along with all the power and abundance of life His Spirit offers—is the ultimate answer. We ask Him for bread, for money, for a spot on the team, for an acceptance letter. And He may give us those things. He is that kind of Father. But sometimes we are so fixated on our thirst that we are blind to how our requests may be shortsighted and shortchanging. We want rain. Mere water. And given the severity and length of whatever drought we've faced, that's an understandable request. But before that, He wants to give us something else. Something more. Someone living.

A fresh revelation and experience of His Spirit. His fire.

This is what you really want. I promise you it is.

"Sometimes our deepest desire does not truly reflect our deepest need."

**#ELIJAHBIBLESTUDY**

## DAY TWO
# No More Hopscotch

---

*"Then Elijah approached all the people and said, 'How long will you waver between two opinions? If the LORD is God, follow him. But if Baal, follow him.' But the people didn't answer him a word."*

**1 KINGS 18:21, CSB**

---

Sometimes a single question or statement, inserted at just the right instant, can halt and hush all other conversation. Suddenly there's nothing more to say.

*A mic drop, per se.*

That's what Elijah did at this pivotal moment on the crest of Mount Carmel. High stakes and high tension were thick in the early morning air. Nearly a thousand pagan prophets had gathered in attendance, along with the entire assembled nation of Israel. It was setting up to be an all-out spiritual throw down. And into this hive of energy and anticipation, Elijah lobbed an all-or-nothing question, right there into the center of his countrymen—a question that we are required to answer as well.

> "How much longer will you waver, hobbling between two opinions?"
>
> **1 KINGS 18:21, NLT**

Elijah's question is so important and foundational to what this whole episode on the mountain is meant to communicate that I'm settling in on this verse today and tomorrow to allow extra opportunity for self-examination. So pause just a moment before moving on.

Let Elijah's question penetrate the depth of your soul in this moment.

## HOW LONG WILL YOU WAVER BETWEEN TWO OPINIONS?

One way to begin determining where your allegiances truly lie is to survey where you commit the bulk of your resources—your time, your words, your talents. For example, what would a scroll through your social media accounts reveal about your consistency in being loyal to God's claim on your heart and life? Or how have you prioritized time with Christ compared to your time practicing a certain sport or doing a favorite hobby? I've left plenty of space here for you to reflect and journal.

The original Hebrew word that translates to the English word "waver" is *pacach* (pronounced "paw-SAKH"), a verb meaning "to pass over, spring over, to skip."[1] Think of it as a light-footed bounce, a step that's rarely steady and firm. Or picture it as an old-fashioned game of hopscotch (hop, skip, jump).

Though Jezebel had worked hard to eradicate the worship of Yahweh altogether, the people simply possessed too much history with the Lord to abandon their affiliation to Him entirely. They knew what they *should* do. They knew where their spiritual allegiances *should* lie. But they were conflicted. They'd set their worship of Baal beside their worship of God. Like commuter trains running on twin tracks, their loyalties were divided: one leg of faith here, another leg of faith there, hopping back and forth as convenience and cultural pressures dictated.

Because of the spiritual corruption and weakness in Ahab's (and Jezebel's) leadership, the people of Israel believed they were in a bind. They felt that they needed to show at least outward honor to Baal if they hoped to placate their pagan rulers and fly under the radar of governmental judgment.

But Elijah—Yahweh's spokesperson and representative—would not allow for this watered-down allegiance to continue. He insisted on a clear, exclusive, unadulterated choice.

### "HOW LONG WILL YOU WAVER ... IF THE LORD IS GOD, FOLLOW HIM. BUT IF BAAL, FOLLOW HIM."

*One commentator calls Elijah's statement a "dramatized form of the first commandment."[2] Turn to Exodus 20:3 to remind yourself of what this commandment entails. How does Elijah's question mirror this primary law?*

*It's also akin to a question that Joshua posed during another phase of Israel's journey. Turn to Joshua 24:15, and write it verbatim below.*

Joshua's question makes clear that a person's choice to play spiritual hopscotch—dancing from one side to the other, attempting to balance the weight of their loyalty equally between the true God and an illegitimate one—is actually a cancellation of that loyalty altogether.

> "Yahweh must be God alone to us, or He is not our God at all."
>
> #ELIJAHBIBLESTUDY

This kind of disjointed lifestyle keeps us off-balance. When we refuse to let other, idolatrous allegiances fall away, we're left to trip through life, limping along, and tossed around by worldly philosophies and misguided patterns of thinking. Worse, we forget our access to His choicest blessings—the sense of His nearness, the fire of His empowering—reserved only for those who choose to seat Him by Himself on the throne of their lives.

Yahweh must be God alone to us, or He is not our God at all.

The truth is, half obedience to God is actually complete disobedience. "The one who is not with Me is against Me," Jesus said (Matt. 12:30), soon after stating the spiritual truism that a "house divided against itself will not stand" (v. 25). Whatever gray areas may exist in the navigation of our lives, there's nothing but darkness and light in this foundational choice that God and His Word lay out before us. Decide. Take your stand—"with Me" or "against Me."

**Make your own personal observations about the following questions, and then prepare to discuss them with your group:**

1. What makes being a passive, lukewarm follower of Jesus more convenient and acceptable in today's culture?

2. What are some of the dynamics and attitudes emerging in current society that could make it even more difficult for young men and women in future generations to remain unmoved in their allegiance to God?

No more hopscotching. Today is the day of decision. No more riding the fence. No more dancing between allegiances. No more caving to fear or outside pressure. You are a fierce daughter of God with an opportunity to experience—like Elijah did—the stability of being anchored in solid, single-minded devotion to Him. Put aside all other loves (we'll be talking throughout the rest of the week how to do that) and recommit yourself to the one true God of Abraham, Isaac, and Jacob. The God who answers by fire.

*The conviction you may feel after studying through these Scriptures today is God's Spirit at work in your heart. It is actually the sting and burn from that fire falling from heaven, exposing and consuming the illegitimate idols in your life. Don't resist its heat. Don't move away from it to a safer place. Confess what He exposes and let Him do away with those cheapened compromises that lead you to satisfy your desires in godless, unsatisfying places. Let Him be first. Let Him be all. He is always enough.*

"Half obedience to God is actually complete disobedience."

**#ELIJAHBIBLESTUDY**

# DAY THREE
# Say Something

*"Oh, Lord, the great and awesome God, who keeps His covenant and faithfulness for those who love Him and keep His commandments, we have sinned, we have done wrong, and acted wickedly and rebelled ..."*

**DANIEL 9:4b-5**

> *"Elijah approached all the people and said, 'How long will you waver between two opinions? If the LORD is God, follow him. But if Baal, follow him.' But the people didn't answer him a word."*
>
> **1 KINGS 18:21, CSB**

Elijah expected to get a response. He didn't talk just to be heard. The Lord sent this prophet. Therefore, the word that was spoken was from the Lord and was intended to come back in the form of repentant hearts and apologetic responses.

*Revisit the verse we studied yesterday, which appears here in the margin. What did the biblical historian of 1 Kings report about how the people responded to Elijah's question?*

Deafening silence. Icy stillness. Elijah had drawn this line in the sand—"If the LORD is God, follow him. But if Baal, follow him"—and the people said nothing. Not one of them spoke up.

But of course their wordlessness was indeed a loud and clear response. It revealed their apathy, their indifference, their complacency, their overall cluelessness. By saying nothing, they were really saying everything—that their hearts were unstable, their loyalties divided, their minds unmade. They were complicit in the nation's pervasive godlessness by their own silence in regard to it. And apparently, until challenged by Elijah that morning, they'd fully and unthinkingly intended to keep riding out this balancing act for the rest of their lives.

*Where would you say your life gives silent assent to habits or practices that you know are out of line with absolute devotion to God?*

*What makes saying nothing feel like a more acceptable option than speaking up?*

*If one of your classmates or closest friends was asked to describe your allegiance to God, circle which adjective that person might use.*

- Nominal
- Bold
- Complete
- Indifferent

- Obvious
- Quiet
- Dogmatic
- Weak

*Explain your reasons for selecting that word.*

*Are you satisfied with the adjective you chose? Why or why not?*

*Now turn your attention inward. How do you sense God's Spirit pricking your heart about cementing your allegiance to Him until it's absolutely unmistakable to everyone around who knows you?*

*Remember what* **SYNCRETISM** *means? We talked about it briefly in Week One. It's the acceptance and blending of different religious beliefs or practices, creating an ungrounded tolerance for all faith positions, as opposed to upholding the truth as being true no matter what.*

The real danger of our disloyalty to God, whether active or passive, actually goes much deeper than merely the making of a spiritual choice. It's not just a decision with spiritual implications; it's a whole way of life decision.

In ancient Israel, where syncretism ran rampant, exclusive allegiance to Yahweh meant living with a perspective on society that was completely unlike that which the followers of Baal embraced. In a God-centered worldview, when properly understood, all people are equal in relationship to one another, no matter their social status, all equally valuable to one divine King. This is what they and their ancestors had been taught. Yahweh was viewed as the owner of the land and the ultimate leader of the people. *All* the people.

But the followers of Baal saw things differently. Their god legitimized a hierarchical structure and stratification where the king, along with an elite ruling class of the successful, influential, and wealthy, were ascribed with having greater divine connectivity and favor from the gods. Their success was a sign of the gods' approval.

So Elijah's ultimatum to Israel, as one writer surmises, "was not merely which God to serve, but in what social configuration to live in." It meant "enduring the consequences of that choice both economically and socially."[3] In other words, Elijah was asking them to make a decision that would impact every area of their lives, how they navigated their view of others, and how they viewed their own personal success. This ultimatum concerning which God or god they intended to serve would in effect determine their entire worldview.

*Consider the implications of the last several paragraphs. Underline any portions that you see demonstrated or abused in modern-day culture.*

*Now consider it personally. Use the space in the margin to record how a biblical view of God impacts how you live and the decisions you make in areas such as:*

- School
- Dating
- Extra-curriculars

- Friendships
- Civil rights
- Political views

(Discuss two or three of these with a friend you can trust.)

In time, this refusal to secure their allegiances would cost the Northern Kingdom of Israel their existence. Twelve evil kings or so after Ahab, after generations of following "worthless idols"—until, as Scripture says, the people became "worthless themselves" (2 Kings 17:15, CSB)—Samaria fell to the Assyrians. "The LORD removed Israel from his presence just as he had declared through all his servants the prophets" (v. 23)—all those prophets who, like Elijah, had sought from God's people an answer, an acknowledgment of their sinful duplicity, one that would stick for more than a day and a half, one that would lead to a permanent change from this repeated pattern.

*Turn to 2 Kings 17:35-39 and review the consistent instructions, as well as the consistent promises, that God had been giving His people for centuries.*

Now read verses 40-41. Note the summary statement against them:

- They feared and worshiped _____.
- But they also _____ their _____.

Picture yourself with me right now. Sunrise atop Mount Carmel. Hear the words of Elijah echoing off the surrounding cliff formations and cascading down into the valley. As his final syllable fades out of listening range, experience the silence descending over the whole crowd. Feel its heartbeat. Ache from it. And while everyone else around you warily shifts their weight from one foot to the other, be the one who's unwilling to choke down the cry of loyalty to Yahweh. Even if all the rest stand silent, turn your voice into a chorus of one.

*The people didn't answer him a word?*

Not us. Not you and me. Not these two people.

### Together, let's confess the words of the prophet Jeremiah. Why not say them out loud, right now?

"We know our wickedness, LORD, the iniquity of our fathers, for we have sinned against You. Do not despise us, for the sake of Your own name; do not disgrace the throne of Your glory. Remember and do not annul Your covenant with us. Are there any among the idols of the nations who give rain? Or can the heavens grant showers? Is it not You, LORD our God? Therefore we wait for You, For You are the one who has done all these things."

**JEREMIAH 14:20-22**

Amen. Yes, amen.

# DAY FOUR

# You First

---

*"A person's pride will humble him, but a*
*humble spirit will gain honor."*

**PROVERBS 29:23, CSB**

---

*Start today's lesson by reading the following section from our key passage this week (1 Kings 18). It's printed for you below. Here, Elijah was laying out the terms of the contest to all those gathered on Mount Carmel: Israel on one side; the pagan prophets on the other. Underline all the portions that display Elijah's confidence.*

"Let two bulls be given to us. They are to choose one bull for themselves, cut it in pieces, and place it on the wood but not light the fire. I will prepare the other bull and place it on the wood but not light the fire. Then you call on the name of your god, and I will call on the name of the LORD. The God who answers with fire, he is God."

All the people answered, "That's fine."

Then Elijah said to the prophets of Baal, "Since you are so numerous, choose for yourselves one bull and prepare it first. Then call on the name of your god but don't light the fire."

**1 KINGS 18:23-25, CSB**

*After all the people agreed to the terms of the contest, what did Elijah allow the Baalists to do?*

*What reason did he give for it?*

Even though there were other Israelites on Mount Carmel that day, Elijah was the only one who was unapologetic and verbal about his complete allegiance to Yahweh. He was, in essence, outnumbered 850 to 1. He certainly felt that way. "I am the only remaining prophet of the LORD," he said (1 Kings 18:22, CSB). Despite this, he willingly deferred to his adversaries in this contest, allowing them the first opportunity to invoke the fiery response of their god.

The question is: *Why?*—why would he do this? and *How?*—how could he muster up the courage and confidence to do it? With such grand odds at stake and in such a highly intimidating environment, how could he show no signs of concern or worry or insecurity, even while giving his opponents the seeming advantage of going first?

It's because of something he knew—and I mean *really* knew—and it's the one thing I want you to walk away from today's devotional believing and consistently incorporating into your reactions toward the overwhelming circumstances in your life. Here it is:

## THE PERCEIVED ADVANTAGE OF BEING FIRST IS ALWAYS TRUMPED BY THE ACTUAL ADVANTAGE OF HAVING ACCESS TO GOD'S FIRE.

When you know that God is for you, when you know His Spirit lives within you, and when you're convinced (as the gospel says you can be) that His favor and presence rests upon you, you are no longer consumed with insecurity about the odds that may be stacked against you. Neither the "best" nor the "biggest" nor the "first" is any comparison for having God's blessing and backing.

So the real question becomes this:

## DO YOU BELIEVE THAT YOUR GOD IS THE ONE TRUE GOD OR NOT?

Elijah knew the only fire that was going to fall that day would be coming from Yahweh's hand. He *knew* it. That's why an absolute confidence could brim within his heart. His willingness to wait, defer, and lead from a position of humility communicated the assurance of his conviction. He basically said, "You take first; I'll take fire."

This principle we're studying today—about having confidence in God, despite being outnumbered or overwhelmed—can be seen in many different scenarios throughout the Scriptures.

For example, Goliath was much bigger than David, but David had God on his side. "You come to me with a sword and with a spear and with a javelin, but I come to you in the name of the LORD of hosts, the God of the armies of Israel" (1 Sam. 17:45, ESV). Joseph was outnumbered and overpowered by his big brothers, and yet God's favor and blessing rested on him as the younger brother,

"When you know that God is for you, that His Spirit lives within you, and that His favor and presence are upon you, you are no longer consumed with insecurity about the odds that may be stacked against you."

**#ELIJAHBIBLESTUDY**

so that even when they planned and executed evil against Him, God turned it around "for good" (Gen. 50:20).

> *Take a peek at one of my favorite Old Testament examples, Judges 7:2-9, which chronicles the famed beginnings of Gideon's battle against one hundred forty thousand Midianite soldiers.*

- Verse 2: How did the Lord describe Gideon's original army?

- Verses 3-8: Do the math. How many men did Gideon start with? How many did he end up sending home? How many remained to go into battle?

- Verse 9: What was Yahweh's promise to Gideon and his small army?

My favorite portion of this passage is found in that second verse, when God said to Gideon, "The people who are with you are too many for Me to hand Midian over to them" (v. 2). In other words, the more resources Gideon had at his disposal, the less of a victory he would experience. Having more was actually working against him.

Did you catch what I said? Having more worked *against* him!

I'm floored by this. I often wonder how many times I've refused to release things from my life that, at the time, seemed advantageous or even necessary. In hindsight though, I realize they were actually acting as repellents to the fire of heaven that God wanted to give. I continually try to remember what God told Gideon to do: "I will save you with the three hundred men . . . so have all the other people go" (v. 7). Translation? Don't be afraid to have fewer. Don't be afraid to go second. Don't be afraid to look weaker by comparison. *I've got your back, and you've got My favor.* That's all you need on your side to secure the victory.

That's where Gideon got his confidence. Where Elijah got his confidence. Where you and I can get our confidence, too. And when we're confident—with that kind of confidence—we don't need to gather more reinforcements, or go first, or maneuver ourselves into a favorable position for outsmarting and outperforming everybody else. Instead we can walk into any situation with authentic humility, which is one of the key elements that invites the fire of heaven.

Our flesh is so easily tickled toward pride and self-sufficiency that we instinctively lean toward wanting to be first, to be the best, to have the most. So God, in order to curb this tendency of ours, often allows us to enter situations where the odds are tilted against us, where we're liable to experience a frightful twinge of insufficiency. But rather than avoid these moments, be like Elijah—embrace them as an opportunity to practice humility, to defer to others, and to refuse succumbing to insecurity.

Don't back down and run away from hard things. Believe instead that God can do unbelievable things in the face of them.

> As you close today's lesson, read Psalm 73:23-26 and 2 Corinthians 3:4-5. Choose one to write on a note card and place it where you will see it regularly throughout the next week. Ask the Lord to cement its truths into your heart. Then ask Him to help you be able to react, respond, and relate to others with a greater sense of confidence in who He is and what He can accomplish on your behalf.

One of the keys that invites the fire of heaven in our lives is

_____

"Humble yourselves in the presence of the Lord, and He will exalt you."

**JAMES 4:10**

# Stop the Frenzy

---

*"When you pray, do not keep on babbling like pagans, for they think they will be heard because of their many words."*

**MATTHEW 6:7, NIV**

---

If I could choose only one word to describe how the majority of people in our current culture feel on a routine, daily basis, it would be *exhausted*. Next time you ask someone "How are you doing?" and if you're willing to hang around after they've said, "Fine, thank you," *exhaustion* is most likely what you'll hear next.

We're so busy. We're so stretched. We're overwhelmed at the thought of what we already know is coming up in the day ahead of us, before we've even factored in the stuff that we don't even yet know to expect. The constant clawing to accomplish and succeed, to gain attention and followers, has made this society a weary one to live in.

On Mount Carmel, in the ongoing saga of Elijah against the prophets of Baal on Mount Carmel, the pagans took the first opportunity to prove the power of the god they served. And their turn would be marked by the same insane exhaustion that we see marking many of our lives today.

> **Turn back to 1 Kings 18:23-24 where Elijah gave instructions about how the day's proceedings were going to go. Make a list of the four things that each opponent was supposed to do in preparation for the showdown.**
>
> 1. Choose _____ for the sacrifice
> 2. _____ it up into pieces
> 3. Place it on the _____
> 4. Call on _____
>
> **What was each participant told not to do?**

*According to verse 24, how would the winner be determined?*

The God/god who _____ is _____.

Let the games begin.

And now, sit back, relax, and observe the way of pagans—the exhausting methods of those who have no security or confidence in their god and are not able to rest in the knowledge of receiving faithful, loving oversight and care. Notice the difference between Elijah and the idol worshipers in two broad categories: (1) the *time* they invested and (2) the *temperament* they demonstrated.

## TIME

The first part of the morning was taken up with preparing the sacrifice, followed by the beginning of their various rituals for arousing the attention of their god. Remember there were more than eight hundred prophets involved in the ceremony—four hundred fifty prophets of Baal and four hundred prophets of Baal's female consort, Asherah.

*According to the verse in the margin, how long did this activity go on?*

"Then they took the ox which was given them and they prepared it, and they called on the name of Baal from morning until noon ..."

**1 KINGS 18:26a**

They were surely disappointed that Baal was taking so long to respond. But by the time the sun had centered itself in the sky, they were sure it wouldn't be long now. In their convoluted theology, Baal was the god of the sun. In fact, they thought him to be god of the entirety of nature. Surely now that his great, burning presence was directly above them, they believed he was right on the doorstep of igniting the kindling of their sacrifice with his divine power. If he was capable of doing anything, he could certainly—easily!—cause fire to come blazing out of the heavens like a lightning bolt.

So they heightened their antics to capitalize on their supposed midday advantage. Their attempts at gaining the attention of their idol can only be described as an extended period of mass hysteria and chaos. As each hour passed, they escalated the frenzied madness.

Looks like this was turning into an all-day event. And as the sun went down, their level of angst, fear, and wild-eyed desperation went up.

### TEMPERAMENT

*Scan verses 26-29 and write down some of the phrases the Bible uses to describe the fervor of their religious display.*

> *"At noon Elijah mocked them, saying, 'Cry aloud, for he is a god. Either he is musing, or he is relieving himself, or he is on a journey, or perhaps he is asleep and must be awakened.'"*
>
> **1 KINGS 18:27, ESV**

All the noise. The shrieking. The running around and throwing themselves down. Yet it was all to no avail. It generated no response from above. "No voice, no one answered, no one paid attention" (v. 29).

Meanwhile, Elijah and the rest of the people of Israel waited for this chaotic scene to wind down. Elijah even, in a truly humorous moment from Scripture, taunted the pagans from his seat at the picnic table, wondering what could be holding up their precious god from paying them any mind.

The important task for us, more than trying to interpret the wildness of their behavior, is to make sure that our own behavior doesn't mirror it. Since we are not idol worshipers and do not serve an impotent god, our spiritual lives should not be marked by the same exhausting realities that mark theirs.

Now look carefully again at how the last line of 1 Kings 18:26 characterizes the idolaters' activity. Notice that the whole idea in the original text is from the word we learned about a few days ago: *pacach*. Do you see it? All that bouncing around, leaping from one stance to the next. It's the same kind of exhausting, back-and-forth "wavering." It comes from the same root system. The draining, taxing, fatiguing hard work that depicts the existence of those who worship idols was not to be mirrored in the experience of God's people.

A frenzied life is not a faith-filled life.

> **"A frenzied life is not a faith-filled life."**
>
> **#ELIJAHBIBLESTUDY**

Oh, the heartbreaking emptiness of serving a god who not only *won't* respond but *can't*. Every idol we place our trust in—whether entertainment or achievement or relationships or connections or anything else that we expect to satisfy us with meaning and fulfillment—they are all incapable of it. They are all phony gods, and seeking to gain satisfaction from them will leave us exhausted.

We, whose God has given us His Son, who has declared us His own beloved children, and who has demonstrated His utter willingness and capacity to

give us everything we need—beyond what we could ask or think—we should be able to rest and enjoy a sense of inner (and external) contentment in every situation.

*He* doesn't need impressing. And *we* don't need the kind of exhausted existence that a life in step with Him is designed to free us from.

> **In what areas of your life are you most exhausted as you try to get something or someone to satisfy you? Why?**

> **Turn to one or more of the following passages, and jot down next to each reference a principle to be gleaned from what it tells you.**

> **Psalm 135:15-18:** _____

> **Isaiah 44:9-11:** _____

> **Habakkuk 2:18-20:** _____

You have not been called to an exhausting spiritual life—wavering, weaving, overworking, selfishly wanting. You are His beloved daughter. Heir to a great inheritance. You can live in settled confidence. You can adjust from folly to faith. You can apply the hard-learned lessons of the process and rest in His sure provision.

And you can know the fire is sure to come.

> **Confess to your Father any of the ways that you recognize your own life in the example of the idol worshipers on Carmel. Repent of the areas where you've stopped trusting Him, trading faith for doubt, panic, and fear. Then ask His Spirit to empower you to live in a way that's clearly distinct from those who do not know Him. Ask Him to teach you to rest and live in step with the rhythm of grace.**

> "Truly my soul finds rest in God; my salvation comes from him. Truly he is my rock and my salvation; he is my fortress, I will never be shaken"
>
> **PSALM 62:1-2, NIV**

# Carmel

## EXPERIENCING THE AUTHENTIC

 **Fire:** Submitting to God's Power

# Inviting the Fire

One of my favorite worship leaders is Tasha Cobbs Leonard. She is a vocal powerhouse and her ability to lead people into the presence of God is only outmatched by her own integrity, her own grace, and her ministry. One of her older songs that I still listen to very frequently is called Fill Me Up. I love it because it's actually more of a prayer than it is a declaration. It's asking God to provide an overabundance of His Spirit, His grace, His favor and strength, His blessing, and His unhindered presence for every task and every divine assignment that we undertake.

I often find myself humming her song—whether it's when I'm sharing a Bible study with you, or whether it's the ministry task of taking care of growing sons, which is my real job. I want to share one of my favorite lyrics from that song. It says, "You provide the fire, I'll provide the sacrifice."[1]

Listen to the simplicity of that again. It's so simple and yet overwhelmingly powerful. Lord, you prepare the fire, and I'll provide the sacrifice.

We're supposed to prepare our part, which is a worthy sacrifice under the Lord. Then we must trust God to do His part to send a holy fire. My part is to intentionally and carefully and willingly present a whole-hearted offering of my whole self that will be worthy of a holy, almighty Father. And then, I'm supposed to depend on Him and trust that He will meet my offering with a fire that only He should be responsible to ignite and initiate.

You and I are now standing on the pinnacle of Mount Carmel along with Elijah. Here we are at this climactic moment when he is daring the adversaries of Yahweh to persuade their impotent idol to rain down fire from heaven. He sets out the rules right from the start of the competition. He commands each side to prepare a sacrifice, but then he says, "You must not light your own fire. You leave that part to God." And the one who answers by fire, He alone is God.

There it is. The holy sacred element that separates the one true God from all other so called gods, the fire. The fire that falls from heaven.

# Press Play

*The* _____ *that falls from heaven.*

*I don't just want His fire _____ me. I want His fire _____ me.*

# Discuss

**What does it mean that God ignites the fire? Why does it matter who ignites the fire?**

As we look at Elijah's example of intentionally and daily preparing and presenting a sacrifice unto the Lord, we see that he resisted the urge to do what we humans have a difficult time resisting the urge to do. He resisted the urge and refused to manufacture his own fire.

Sister in Christ, do your part, but then let the Father do His. Don't fabricate your own flame, creating some human made attempt of spiritual victory through self-motivation, self-promotion, or emotionalism in our culture of perfectly lit selfies and stage personas. The image of religion and sacred activities can spew smoke signals that make it appear that our lives are rooted in authentic holy flames. But the question for all of us is this, did we light that fire, or did we wait in the presence of God until he sent His fire?

Prepare a worthy sacrifice. Yes, prepare your life, your whole life, as a living sacrifice holy to the Lord. Prepare your time, your talents, your treasures and present them in a way worthy to the Lord. But resist the urge to start your own fire.

*How do Christians attempt to make their lives appear to be filled with a holy fire when in reality it is empty?*

*Read 1 Kings 18:30-36. How was Elijah intentional in the way he rebuilt the altar?*

*Why does God require us to be intentional, not apathetic or half-hearted, in the way we live for Him?*

Instead of prioritizing your time with God, if you're anything like me, you'll wait until the end of the day. And so then you give Him the leftovers that you have in strength and in energy. Sometimes we reserve the best of our efforts and our skills and our attitudes for every place except for God and His people.

We have to have a heart that desires to be intentional, just like Elijah shows us, so that we present an offering upon which the fire of God can fall. Obviously in the Old Testament, the objects of their sacrifice were different. What they would present was different, but now we give ourselves as a living offering, a living sacrifice as unto the Lord. So think of your time, your talents, your gifts, your treasures in that way, and then be intentional.

*How can you be intentional with what God has given you right now?*

I'm going to tell you right now, this kind of intentionality is going to take boldness. In our post-Christian culture, where more and more our entire society is celebrating the things that are out of alignment with the truth of God, you are going to need to be bold. As you may be teased in school for being the one that stands for righteousness and the truth of God and as you're the one that chooses not to be politically correct, you need to know that in that choice to step forward, to be bold, oftentimes that's where the fire of God will meet you.

## Press Play

*Never _____ the power of a _____ _____.*

*Prayer doesn't _____ God. Prayer just _____ all the things He _____ to do for us anyway.*

*After Elijah prayed that prayer, the sky _____ _____, and God _____ down _____.*

# *Discuss*

*What is the purpose of prayer? How might we pray at times to attempt to manipulate God?*

*How do we shift from pretending to live for Christ to actually living for Him with a holy fire?*

## DAY ONE
# An Intentional Sacrifice

*"Therefore, brothers and sisters, in view of the mercies of God, I urge you to present your bodies as a living sacrifice, holy and pleasing to God; this is your true worship."*

**ROMANS 12:1, CSB**

Sister, here we are.

In the fifth week of Bible study. With Elijah on Mount Carmel.

When the fire of God will fall from heaven.

*For more about the fire of God , read Digging Deeper II on page 132.*

The people of Israel had just finished watching the hours-long, vain efforts of the prophets of Baal, with not even a flicker of fire to show for it. And now, it was Yahweh's turn. Elijah knew for a faith-filled fact that the holy, fiery power of Yahweh would soon fall, and his unmitigated confidence in Him was about to be confirmed and revealed.

But first things first. In the next scene to unfold on the mountain, Elijah painstakingly prepared and presented a sacrifice worthy of receiving God's fire. And we must mark it well, because his deliberate, meticulous actions preceding Yahweh's response would demonstrate to everyone—and to us—the significance of paying attention to the way we offer ourselves to God. Offering our whole lives as a "holy and pleasing" acceptable sacrifice becomes a magnet that invites the favor and blessing of God.

> *Turn to 1 Kings 18:30-35. Read it through, and then keep these verses on hand because we'll cover this entire passage today.*
>
> *Beginning in verse 30, what did Elijah do to "the altar of the LORD" that had been torn down. He _____ it.*
>
> *What significant feature does verse 31 detail? What does this element represent?*

Take time to consider the fact that Elijah completely avoided anything that was devoted to the worship of Baal, even in part. He preferred instead doing the hard, sweat-producing work of rebuilding an altar where sacrifices had once been made to God, prior to the building of the temple (see 1 Kings 3:2), rather than the ease of using a well-built framework that had been dedicated to idols. To him, the extra effort was worth it.

Equally telling is the fact that Elijah also refused to start from scratch, building something brand new. The prophet's goal was not to introduce a new form of worship but to respect Yahweh's history with His people. But in its state, this altar that Elijah chose to use was in no condition to receive God's fire. It needed repair. It needed rebuilding.

And so he rebuilt it with *twelve* stones. Not eleven. Not thirteen. *Twelve*—an important number in Israel's history. The twelve stones symbolized the twelve tribes and would have pointed to the conquest of Canaan, including the property right here in what was once known as God's glorious promised land. It was spiritual heritage and inheritance all in one, surging through the hearts of a nation who'd forgotten what they were all about—all because of Elijah's thoughtful and intentional choice to select *twelve* scattered stones and wedge them tightly together for the foundation of the altar. His discerning and deliberate actions at this juncture not only emphasized Yahweh's covenant but would also remind them of something more.

Elijah's precision and attention to detail continued with another series of deliberate steps, each one proving to be more stunning and surprising than what he'd done at first with the twelve stones.

*An extravagant gift may impress people, but an intentional gift is what impresses God.*

*Check back in with 1 Kings 18 now and describe what happened next:*

- *Verse 32: What did he create around the altar?*

- *Verse 33: What did he arrange on top of the altar?*

- *Verse 34: What did he pour over the altar?*

- *Verse 35: What was the final appearance of the altar?*

Imagine the people's disbelief, having lived every day for the last three years treating each drop of water as a precious commodity, now seeing it sloshed over the altar until it could hold no more. If water was what they'd come to Mount Carmel for, they hadn't come to see it wasted and poured out on the ground!

But nothing was being wasted here. Everything was intentional. The seemingly ridiculous abundance of water—once, twice, three times more unthinkable with each thorough dousing—was intended to underscore the miraculous nature of what was about to occur. It would draw unmistakable recognition to the power and full authority that belonged to God and God alone.

> *Reread and underline the last line of the previous paragraph. Then, using details from the verse in the margin (1 Kings 18:38), write a few sentences on how Elijah's addition of water contributed to the "unmistakable recognition" of Yahweh's power.*

*"Then the fire of the LORD fell and consumed the burnt offering and the wood, and the stones and the dust; and it licked up the water that was in the trench."*

**1 KINGS 18:38**

The response is what we want. Our heart's desire is that our whole lives be a worthy offering that produces "a fragrance of Christ to God" (2 Cor. 2:15).

Our offerings to the Lord today are not built and composed of such things as oxen, stone altars, and water-filled moats. But as the apostle Paul spelled out plainly in Romans, we do present ourselves to God as "a living sacrifice"— "holy and pleasing"—as being indicative of our "true worship" (Rom. 12:1, CSB). The sacrifice is our full, living, breathing selves—our time, our talents, our treasures, our bodies (which are temples of the Holy Spirit). We surrender them each day to Him as instruments for His glory.

But notice Paul didn't just tell us we *must* do it; he told us *how* to do it, in a way that is "holy and pleasing" to God. This kind of total-life offering requires thoughtfulness—a consistent intentionality on our part. It won't happen if we're haphazard or only casually attentive, nor can we offer ourselves begrudgingly or resentfully. Instead, Elijah's example should compel us to examine our own lives today and ask questions like these:

• Are we conscious and intentional in honoring our Father with the output of our hours, decisions, priorities, attitudes, and actions, or do we leave it all to chance?

- Do we take time to carefully consider how we can create margin for His glory to be glaringly displayed in our lives?

Because if we are looking for the God of fire to answer by fire, we need to be as diligent as Elijah in preparing the sacrifice to receive it.

*For each category below, try accurately estimating where you currently fall on the scale. Obviously your answer could be different next week or next month as you continue letting God deal with your heart in these matters. But use this exercise to gain a daringly honest perspective on how you're doing right now. Rate yourself from 1 to 10—with 1 being poor and 10 being excellent.*

## ~ time ~

*How well are you prioritizing your time, making valuable use of it to God? (Do you prioritize the things that are important to Him in your schedule, or do you just hope they'll happen?)*

| 1 | 2 | 3 | 4 | 5 | 6 | 7 | 8 | 9 | 10 |
|---|---|---|---|---|---|---|---|---|----|

*Why did you choose this rating?*

## ~ talents ~

*How faithfully are you using your gifts and abilities to honor God and fulfill your purpose? (Do you reserve your best self for everyone else except the workings of the house of God and encouraging the people of God?)*

| 1 | 2 | 3 | 4 | 5 | 6 | 7 | 8 | 9 | 10 |
|---|---|---|---|---|---|---|---|---|----|

*Why did you choose this rating?*

### ~ Treasures ~

*How deliberately are you investing the resources God has given you to enhance the kingdom of God?*

1    2    3    4    5    6    7    8    9    10

---

*Why did you choose this rating?*

As you allow the Holy Spirit to examine your life and encourage you toward intentionality in these areas, remember that you are a beloved daughter with no need to earn your Father's approval and blessing. You have been saved by faith, not by works. Your relationship with Him is established, and it will endure.

So relax. Presenting yourself to the Lord is an exercise in gratitude. It's something you can sustain, not by tireless effort, but only by walking in step to the rhythm of His grace and depending on the empowerment of His Spirit. Seek Him in prayer and ask for insight on how He wants you to adjust your life to best honor Him. He will give you the clarity, and He will also give you the desire to please Him, "for it is God who is at work in you, both to desire and to work for His good pleasure" (Phil. 2:13).

He wants His Spirit to consume you, and for His fruit and gifts to be expressed through you, so that your life becomes a billboard that shows forth the glory of God.

# DAY TWO

# Completely His

---

*"The eyes of the LORD roam throughout the earth,*
*so that He may strongly support those*
*whose heart is completely His."*

**2 CHRONICLES 16:9a**

---

Yesterday we saw Elijah's commitment to prepare a worthy sacrifice, but the lessons we learn from his example on Mount Carmel don't stop there.

**Turn to 1 Kings 18:36. Reading just the opening phrase, how does your Bible describe the action Elijah took after preparing his sacrifice on the altar?**

*Elijah _____ _____.*

Different versions say he "came up" or "walked up" or "came near" or "approached." I like how the New International Version says it: "Elijah stepped forward." Stepped forward and away from the crowd. Stepped up and out on his own. Stepped into a position of leading the people instead of melding seamlessly with them. He created distance between himself and the halfhearted followers of Yahweh, and he directly contradicted the prophets of Baal.

Before the fire fell, Elijah "stepped forward" in boldness and courage.

This kind of unapologetic individuality was rare in Elijah's day, just like it's rare in ours. While other followers of Yahweh were present on the mountain, and still others who'd not bent a knee to worship Baal were in hiding, running scared from Jezebel's tyranny, Elijah was different. In a time when being clear and unashamed about your commitment to Yahweh could cost someone his life, Elijah was so committed to his God that the comfort and safety of sameness just wouldn't do. This feature of Elijah's ministry is one of the living, breathing hallmarks that challenges me the most.

Pay careful attention now. In order to be positioned for the fire Yahweh was sending, Elijah had to distance himself from his fellow countrymen and his fellow followers of Yahweh.

At some point one or both of these dynamics will be required of us too.

As the Spirit of God challenges and convicts us toward fearlessness and unashamed commitment, we will frequently need to create distance between ourselves and "our people." Sometimes, in order to be in wholehearted allegiance to our God, we'll have to move away from friendships and relationships. In this post-Christian era, "stepping forward" will require separation from many who may possess similar beliefs as ours, but who have become apathetic, lukewarm, and watered-down in their commitment to God and His truth.

The kind of boldness that is unashamed of the pure gospel, committed to the inerrancy of God's Word, and unwavering in His standard of holiness will increasingly necessitate a rejection of political correctness and social acceptance. The most stubborn deterrent to receiving the full expression of God's presence and blessing in our lives is the pressure to pursue conformity and acceptance over obedience.

*How have you recently sensed God leading you to step out in bold faith and belief that will require a clear line of delineation between yourself and "your people"?*

*How could you create the kind of Christian environment where people feel less held back by the fears and pressures of peers? Share your answer with your group the next time you meet.*

*Now let's look again at Elijah's comment in 1 Kings 18:22, printed in the margin. What does this statement tell us about his personal sentiments as he stood on Mount Carmel?*

**"POST-CHRISTIAN"** *culture is one in which a society that once based the majority of its shared ethics and beliefs on a biblical worldview have now marginalized those convictions behind other systems of thought and practice.*

*"Elijah said to the people, 'I alone am left as a prophet of the LORD, while Baal's prophets are 450 men.'"*

**1 KINGS 18:22**

*Given the details in 1 Kings 18:4, 20 and 19:18, what was the true reality?*

Elijah's wholehearted allegiance was so rare that he felt like he was completely alone, despite the fact that he was surrounded by thousands of others from his own kin and spiritual community. He was the only one standing *here*. He was the only one who "stepped forward" *like this*. He may not have been technically alone, but he sure *felt* like he was. There was no encouragement, no one to stand by him on that mountain. And you'll likely feel the same way, too, whenever you take a bold stance in your faith—on your school's campus, in your neighborhood, on the athletic field, as part of that organization, or in that family dynamic.

And yet, even as you gear up for the challenge in your own set of unique personal dynamics, remember that there are others—a remnant of us believers who are unashamed and unapologetic. You are not alone even when you feel like you might be. Always remember that your Father has been preparing you for this. The stages of development that we've seen unfolding in Elijah's experience point to it. Every juncture in his life had been designed to cement the boldness of his spiritual backbone so that he'd be fortified to stand in the lone spotlight of Carmel.

Think back:

- In *Gilead*, shepherding for lonesome hours on end in the hills and pasturelands
- Under the hot sun at *Cherith*, with only ravens bringing him food
- In *Zarephath*, as an outsider in a foreign land

In each place, Elijah's whole life had been instructed and informed by the lessons of solitude. God had been his companion. His trusted friend. When no one else was around to engage in conversation. He'd learned from hard experience that there was no place he could ever be in the whole wide world and not be in the holy, protective presence of his almighty God.

> "Turn your loneliness into solitude, and your solitude into prayer."[2]
>
> —ELISABETH ELLIOT

*How might have previous seasons of forced or voluntary solitude prepared you for the lifestyle of bold separation that is required of you right now?*

Let the powerful words of 2 Chronicles 16:9 foster an eager anticipation in you as you make the hard decisions necessary to step forward with boldness:

> "The eyes of the LORD roam throughout the earth, so that He may strongly support those whose heart is completely His."

**2 CHRONICLES 16:9**

For Elijah, moments after stepping forward, the "strong support" of Yahweh would fall from an open heaven. And as we step forward, our God will do the same for us.

Pray this:

> *Lord, forgive me for the times when I have chosen the acceptance of my peers over my allegiance to You. Forgive me for melding in seamlessly instead of taking a stand for Your truth. I ask You to empower me by Your Spirit to have a boldness and courage that will not bend in the face of adversity and pressure. My heart is wholly Yours. Show me today what it means to live like it. Give me the spirit of Daniel, Caleb, Esther, and Elijah so that I am unashamed, that I am unwilling to be a nominal, lukewarm believer. I want to step forward, out and away from the crowd, and honor You with my whole life. In Jesus' name, amen.*

# Simple Prayer

*"When you pray, do not keep on babbling like
pagans, for they think they will be heard because
of their many words."*

**MATTHEW 6:7, NIV**

It's already been a long day on Mount Carmel.

It started civilly enough, with an agreement on Elijah's terms of engagement.
But then it got rowdy. It got ugly. It got bloody.

Before finally it got quiet. Quiet enough to hear a pagan prophet's
pin-sized belief system drop—belief in a lifeless, voiceless, fire-less god that
they'd pinned all their prayers on.

Then up stepped Elijah—intentionally, boldly—yet simply and prayerfully.

> "LORD, God of Abraham, Isaac and Israel, today let it be known
> that You are God in Israel and that I am Your servant, and that
> I have done all these things at Your word. Answer me, LORD,
> answer me, so that this people may know that You, LORD, are
> God, and that You have turned their heart back."

**1 KINGS 18:36-37**

Last week we studied the increasingly wild pleading that had taken the prophets
of Baal all day long to put into words. Today let's look at how the same request
took Elijah all of twenty seconds. He spoke it in a prayer that was completely
empty of high volume or theatrics or worked-up manipulation, like the pagans'
prayers had been. It comprised about sixty words, when translated into the
English language. His confidence in the ability and authority of Yahweh was
so complete that his prayer reverberated with a powerful simplicity, one
which stood in stark opposition to those who did not know God.

*Look at the terms used to describe the pleas of Baal's prophets from 1 Kings 18 listed in the margin. Underline the main descriptive words in each verse.*

*Think about the way you tend to relate to God. Does your temperament in prayer generally bear more resemblance to the panic of the prophets of Baal, or to the easy trust of the prophet Elijah?*

*How would you say that the confident tone of Elijah's prayer was influenced by what He'd been through in the barrenness of Gilead, the loneliness of Cherith, and the deprivation of Zarephath? What had he learned about God in each place?*

*"Called on the name of Baal from morning until noon."*
**1 KINGS 18:26a**

*"Limped about the altar"* **(v. 26b)**

*"Cried out with a loud voice, and cut themselves"* **(v. 28)**

*"Raved until the time of the offering of the evening sacrifice"* **(v. 29)**

Each unique season of Elijah's journey had given the prophet an opportunity to experience Yahweh in a distinctive way—as a provider, a covenant keeper, a protector, and a life-giver. The consistency of his ongoing friendship with his God supported this intense moment on Carmel. He didn't need to overcompensate by filling the air with superfluous words. Confident trust had been cemented during these three years. His prayer on Mount Carmel was rooted in relationship, and that's where our prayers can be rooted as well.

Too often we tend to think the only way to get God to move is to pray louder, pray longer, pray harder—to pray as if we're hunting for the right magic words, especially if significant time passes and our wait to see God respond continues. And too often when praying in group settings (as Elijah was doing), our goal is mainly to impress people with our flowery grasp of spiritual vocabulary.

But Elijah's prayer wasn't driven by panic or public approval. Even with the high stakes atop Mount Carmel, he simply rooted his prayer in three important end results. He said, Lord, *answer me so that ...*

1. You will be glorified.

2. My relationship with You will be affirmed.

3. The people's hearts will be turned back to you.

## 1. LORD, ANSWER ME SO THAT YOU ...

——————— ———— ——————————.

*Using the text of Elijah's prayer on the previous page or from your own copy of the Bible (1 Kings 18:36-37), write out the portion (or portions) that underscores the purpose of God being glorified.*

The ultimate goal of our prayers and requests should mirror Elijah's example. Even as we pray about the most practical aspects of life, the ultimate end goal must be to highlight God. To draw attention to Him, not us. To magnify Him, not us. Reframing our priorities in prayer around this goal will shift much of what we ask Him for and how we approach Him in our asking.

So take inventory of your prayer life today. If you cannot see a clear tie between what you're asking God to do and how He'll be glorified in doing it, you are out of step with the overarching goal of Jesus Himself—namely, "that the Father may be glorified" (John 14:13). If you recognize that you are not in sync with Him in this area, ask His Spirit to adjust the posture of your heart and the priority of your prayers.

## 2. LORD, ANSWER ME SO THAT ...

——————— —————————————— ————
——————— ———— ———— ——————————.

*Refer back to Elijah's prayer. Write out the portion that speaks to the motive behind his request.*

Receiving Yahweh's validation was his chief goal. The highest affirmation he could receive was that of being Yahweh's representative.

So in prayer, after asking God to glorify Himself, Elijah then entreated Him to affirm their relationship. He wanted people to see that his ambitions, endeavors, and pursuits through the years had not been self-motivated or self-created. None of this "troubling," if that's what Ahab insisted on calling it, had been driven by personal agenda or vindication. Elijah had been on a divinely mandated assignment all along. He was God's servant. His ambassador. And now, everyone would know it.

## 3. LORD, ANSWER ME SO THAT …

_____ _____ _____ _____ _____

_____ _____ _____ _____.

*Last time. Write out the portion of Elijah's prayer that reflects this part of his appeal.*

God's desire, even when judgment is warranted, is that people return to Him. No matter who they are or what they've done.

This is God's heart. He wants His people—He wants you and me—responding to Him, *returning* to Him. We can always know we're praying His heart when we, like Elijah, pray for someone to "turn their heart back again."

Make this simple, heartfelt message a driving motivator behind your prayers: softened hearts, changed minds, and redirected ambitions.

The three important elements we've looked at today form a sturdy foundation for simple, powerful, effective praying. As you mature and develop in your relationship with God, let them guide your conversations with Him.

*In closing today, consider two or three of the most pressing requests that you've been making to the Lord recently. What are you praying for?*

*Now examine your requests in light of the three objectives in Elijah's prayerful example. Over the next few days, for each request, on separate sheets of paper, craft short prayers that align with what you've studied today. Moving forward, use what you've written as a guideline to reframe your prayer life. Confess any way that you've slipped into the panicked, frantic tone of those who do not have confidence in the true and powerful living God. Ask Him to give you wisdom on how to cultivate an effective prayer life that is laced with peace, trust, and the goal of magnifying Him.*

# The Fire Falls

---

*"Then the fire of the LORD fell and consumed the burnt offering*
*and the wood, and the stones and the dust; and it licked up*
*the water that was in the trench."*

**1 KINGS 18:38**

---

We have a lovely fireplace in our home, which I enjoy nearly every day after the heat of Texas summer has given way to fall and winter. I slip into our living room on most mornings, pull the lever that opens the flue into the chimney, light a long-stemmed match, and touch it to the lowest point of the gas logs. Within moments I'm bathed in warmth and shimmering light.

But as pretty as it looks and feels, that's about all a fire can do when I'm the one who lights it. Natural fire is limited. It all depends on me. I decide when the time is right for it. And if I can't get it to start for some reason, it's on me to figure out what I'm doing wrong or what needs to be reworked. It's in my hands. I'm responsible for it. And even after I get it going, it only burns temporarily until I make the decision to start it up again, from the bottom—my only access point for lighting it.

This is what distinguishes a man-made fire from God's supernatural fire.

> **Look again at 1 Kings 18:23, printed in your margin. What did Elijah tell the people he would deliberately avoid doing to his sacrifice?**

> *"I will prepare the other ox and lay it on the wood, and I will not put a fire under it."*
>
> **1 KINGS 18:23**

Consider Elijah's proactive efforts that we've studied over the past three days. He reverently and intentionally prepared his sacrifice. He stepped out boldly from the silent masses. Then he offered up the simplicity of his believing prayer. But what he did *not* do was come anywhere near that altar bearing the torch of his own fire. He understood that lighting the fire would be to encroach upon margin that belonged to Yahweh alone. His own self-ignited fire would mean nothing. A self-cultivated fire would prove nothing.

Believer, remember that the fire of God comes *down*, not up. Down from on high. God lights His fire *Himself*—lights it *with* Himself. God's Spirit enters our soul, stirring in us a holy fervor—first at the moment of our salvation, then more and more as we continue living in alignment with Him and as we continue walking in yielded surrender to Him. He graces us with the intangible yet unmistakable mark of His presence on our lives.

God's fire is the fire we need. Not our fire. His fire.

> **What are some ways we try to kindle our own fire as Christians through emotions, self-promotion, or religious activity? What does that look like in your own life?**

> **What happens to our peace and spiritual contentment when we strive after those things consistently and unsuccessfully?**

Finally, it happened:

> "The fire of the LORD fell and consumed the burnt offering and the wood, and the stones and the dust; and it licked up the water that was in the trench."

**1 KINGS 18:38**

> **In the verse above, underline the elements that God's holy fire consumed.**

It completely consumed the expected things. But it also consumed things that don't usually burn. Solid rock, for example—those twelve stones that corresponded to the twelve tribes of Israel, reinforcing the promise-keeping power of His unbreakable covenant. The fire of God also "licked up" the water. And suddenly, in an instant, those thirsty Israelites—who'd come here thinking only of quenching their thirst after 1,277 days without rain—weren't thinking about that at all anymore.

"God's Spirit enters our soul, stirring in us a holy fervor—first at the moment of our salvation, then more and more as we continue living in alignment with Him and as we continue walking in yielded surrender to Him."

#ELIJAHBIBLESTUDY

"Believer, refuse to light your own fire."

#ELIJAHBIBLESTUDY

> "When all the people saw this, they fell on their faces; and they said, 'The Lord, He is God; the Lord, He is God!'"

**1 KINGS 18:39**

Because that's what the fire of God does. It draws glorious attention to Him and Him alone.

That's why I want it. That's why we need it. That's why He sends it—so that regular humans like you and me can become living, breathing billboards of His presence, and so that we can know what it's like to walk in divine power in everything we do. As we go throughout the rhythm of our daily lives with the presence of God's Spirit oozing out of us—His fruit, His gifts, His goodness, His power—the people in our sphere of influence will see the witness of His Spirit upon us and be compelled to declare, "The LORD, he is God! The LORD, he is God!" Mere talent, hard work, or busyness cannot produce this type of responsive effect.

As I write this lesson to you, I am startlingly aware of this holy reality in my own life and ministry. As my mind is frantically attempting to digest and clearly deliver all the content I've studied and the biblical insight I've tried to glean, I realize my best attempt at this work will be fruitless if God's Spirit doesn't rest His hand upon it. We will both have wasted our time—a series of weeks for you, and a couple of consecutive years for me—if the fire doesn't fall, if the blessing of God does not anoint these devotionals so that their messages are seared within your heart by the Holy Spirit Himself. And so I've recognized (and confessed to Him) my tendency to overwork and under-pray. To overproduce and under-consecrate.

But more and more, I'm learning that holiness and godly priorities will produce what all my extra hours of work never could. That's what I dearly, desperately want. I want the unmistakable mark of God's presence to rest here with me, not only when I'm writing or teaching, but all the time in all the regular rhythms of daily life.

I know you want this too. And our Father offers this experience through His manifest presence with us. Daily. Moment by moment. So let's look to Elijah's example, doing our part as we trust God to do His.

1.   PRESENT YOUR FULL SELF TO GOD—your time, talents and treasures—as a living sacrifice. Not haphazardly, but intentionally and thoughtfully.

2.   BE UNASHAMED—public and bold in your allegiance to Him.

3.   COMMIT TO THE SPIRITUAL DISCIPLINES that cultivate an ongoing, vibrant relationship with God: prayer, Bible reading, humility, and surrender.

Sister, there is grace for these lifestyle choices and patterns. He Himself will walk alongside you as you choose this framework for your life. So don't feel burdened by a spiritual to-do list. Instead relax and enjoy your friendship with God in these consistent ways.

He is for you, and His fire is already falling down upon you.

# Keep the Fire Going

*"Do not let one of them escape."*

**1 KINGS 18:40b**

The previous owners of our current home left behind an outdoor fire pit. I was so glad to see that it was still in the backyard when we moved in. Every so often when we have the time, we'll sit around it on the back patio with metal sticks in hand, roasting marshmallows for s'mores.

I'll never forget the first time we tried to use it. We were so excited. Fire, outdoors, under a blanketing sky—like the country in the city. But no matter what my husband did to kindle that dim flicker of light into a roaring fire that night, nothing worked. He tried several different tricks of his, even resorting to using some starter squares, but still no fire.

That's when we figured out the problem. *The wood was damp.* A thunderstorm the previous night had dropped a good dousing on our uncovered stack of firewood. We knew that. But it hadn't seemed damp to the touch. After seventeen hours of drying out, we figured it would be more than able to burn by now. But it wasn't. The only way we were going to keep and cultivate any fire in the fire pit that night was to get rid of the firewood that was working against it.

Entirely. Log by log.

All of it.

I thought of that evening as I was studying the closing scene of Elijah's confrontation with the prophets of Baal. The glorious fire had come down on Mount Carmel, and the crowd had been awestruck with wonder. Israel's people fell to the ground in worship, while the prophets of Baal stood by.

The spiritual fire had been ignited, but Elijah's assignment was not yet complete. These holy flames of revival needed the right atmosphere in order to keep burning. Anything and everything working against it needed to be removed. Completely.

*It can be difficult to reconcile the grace and goodness of Yahweh with His command to annihilate an entire people group. But remember, He had delayed justice for their rebellion, giving them opportunity for repentance before deeming their cup of iniquity full (see Gen. 15:16; Jonah 3:4) and releasing a divine judgment.*

Elijah said to them, "Seize the prophets of Baal; do not let one of them escape." So they seized them; and Elijah brought them down to the brook Kishon, and slaughtered them there.

**1 KINGS 18:40**

Sound extreme? Yes. But this severe effort was a required element of Elijah's assignment. And it will be ours if we want to cultivate the fire. We must annihilate anything and everything that keeps the fire of God's Spirit from burning brightly and continuously in our lives.

*Before you move forward, consider any habit, attitude, unmanaged desire, or illegitimate relationship that you've allowed to "escape" and go unattended. What are these things that dull your passion and zeal for Jesus? Below, begin an honest list of the things in your life that (1) do not foster God's fire in you or (2) actively contribute to its diminished fervor.*

Picture the sight of these thousands of Israelites in the foreground, falling on their faces and declaring, "The LORD, he is God! The LORD, he is God!" (v. 39), while those hundreds of prophets of Baal stood in shock, unyielding in the background. The stark contrast made their irreverence clear. They still refused to abandon their mission. And Elijah knew if they escaped—even one of them—they would continue to be what F. B. Meyer called "agents of apostasy."[3] It would only be a matter of time before idol worship threaded its way back into the full tapestry of Israel's fabric. He could not let that happen.

And neither can we. For the past two weeks of our Bible study, we've stood on Mount Carmel and we've seen fire rain down from heaven. I'm praying our time here has stirred a fervor in your heart, just like it's done in mine. From this point forward, as we continue to yield to the work of the Holy Spirit, our assignment is to cooperate with Him—"to fan into flame the gift of God" (2 Tim. 1:6, ESV)—by cultivating that relationship through His Word and prayer, and by proactively severing our own "prophets of Baal" who, left unchecked, will dampen the flame.

*Finish your week of Bible study by prayerfully reading through the following passage from Paul in Galatians 5, seeing how the tendencies of the flesh actively work against the work of the Spirit.*

For the desire of the flesh is against the Spirit, and the Spirit against the flesh; for these are in opposition to one another, in order to keep you from doing whatever you want. But if you are led by the Spirit, you are not under the Law. Now the deeds of the flesh are evident, which are: sexual immorality, impurity, indecent behavior, idolatry, witchcraft, hostilities, strife, jealousy, outbursts of anger, selfish ambition, dissensions, factions, envy, drunkenness, carousing, and things like these, of which I forewarn you, just as I have forewarned you, that those who practice such things will not inherit the kingdom of God.

**GALATIANS 5:17-21**

*Now in the words of Elijah, refuse to "let one of them escape." Circle any actions of the flesh listed in the Galatians passage that the Holy Spirit is asking you to seize and slaughter.*

*Who are some people in your circle of influence that you can enlist to help hold you accountable in these areas?*

As you begin to think proactively about how you can follow through, don't slip into worry or a sense of being overwhelmed. Rest and trust. God's Spirit lives in you. He sent the fire, and He will keep it tended. He will give you clarity on how to honor His instructions, as well as the courage to keep going. Then as you commit to the progressive, systematic annihilation of these idols, you will open up the way for God's blessings in your experience.

Just ask godly Elijah. Or you can even ask godless Ahab.

Either one of them could tell you ...

## RAIN IS COMING.

# The Holy Spirit and Fire

Throughout the Old Testament, fire symbolized the manifest presence of the Lord among humanity, not only with Elijah on Mount Carmel but in varying locations and time periods.

Take, for example, God's appearance to Moses from within a burning bush in the desert of Horeb (Ex. 3:2), the fire that fell while Moses and his brother Aaron were serving in the tabernacle (Lev. 9:23-24), and the fire that consumed the sacrifices on the altar when Solomon dedicated the temple (2 Chron. 7:1). In each case, and many others, fire was the tangible representation of Yahweh's nearness and a sign of His approval and acceptance. His presence rendered the soil holy, and everyone in the vicinity was compelled to fall to the ground in reverence. Flesh trembled as Yahweh's holy fire purified, refined, directed, and consumed. These flames could not be crafted by the skillful hands of craftsmen, nor could they be conjured up through the impressive wisdom of kings. The fire was a divine gift, initiated and offered by God alone.

This symbolism continued into the New Testament, where fire is often tied to the ministry of the Holy Spirit in the life of a believer, beginning on the Day of Pentecost (Acts 2). As one scholar summarized, "The zeal of service, the flame of love, the fervour of prayer, the earnestness of testimony, the devotion of consecration, the sacrifice of worship, and the igniting-power of influence are attributable to the Spirit."[4]

To be clear, the Holy Spirit was given to you and me as a gift of our salvation:

> "In Him, you also, after listening to the message of truth, the gospel of your salvation—having also believed, you were sealed in Him with the Holy Spirit of the promise, who is a first installment of our inheritance, in regard to the redemption of God's own possession, to the praise of His glory."
> **EPHESIANS 1:13-14**

As Christ followers, the Holy Spirit is in us. All of Him. But He is only reflected upon and through us to the extent that we allow Him to be. By this I mean that only those who choose a lifestyle of yielded obedience have the opportunity to walk in the full expression of His work in their lives.

We know from Scripture, for instance, that we can "grieve" the Holy Spirit (Eph. 4:30-32), and that we can "quench" the fire of the Spirit from burning brightly in us (1 Thess. 5:19). But as we continue to yield to Him—by heeding His conviction, relying on Him for daily empowerment, and cultivating a fervent friendship—we are "filled with the Spirit" (Eph. 5:18) until His presence overflows in our actions, attitudes, and ambitions. His fruit and His gifts become outworked through our lives. We are graced with His visible favor and empowerment. Our efforts are no longer fueled by mere talent and sweat equity, but they become marked by a divine approval that reverberates with the Father's applause. This is how our whole lives become infused and saturated with purpose, glorifying to the Father, and able to bear eternal fruit. As we follow Elijah's example of humility and integrity, and as we intentionally present a "living sacrifice" of our whole selves to God (Rom. 12:1), we invite the fire of God's presence to consume us.

With our achievement-oriented culture of perfectly-lit selfies and staged personas, it can be easy to assume a veneer of religion and pseudo-sacred activity that appears to spew smoke signals of authentic holy flames. But we must resist the urge to mask any lack of authentic intimacy with God by fabricating our own false flames through emotionalism and self-promotion. His fire is what we need if we expect to live up to our calling and experience the freedom of serving others with selfless joy and real power. Yes, we must do our part diligently (prepare the sacrifice), but then we leave room for the Father to do His (ignite the fire).

Time and eternity will draw a clear distinction between what He has done and what we have manufactured on our own. If the fire is not authentic—if it is by our "might" and our "power" but not by His "Spirit" (Zech. 4:6)—it will eventually flicker and fail.

# Horeb

## FEAR, FATIGUE, AND A FUTURE

 **Fire:** Submitting to God's Power

# Do You Hear What I Hear?

*In the Old Testament, God sent prophets to His people to be His voice. They were His mouthpiece, and they spoke clearly from Him. The prophets were the ones who presented the truth of God and revealed the standard of God in order to call people back from their waywardness and back from their rebellion. The prophets were sent to remind people that God is still who He says He is and that He would still accomplish everything that He said He would accomplish.*

*Do you understand that in our culture, right here and now, we need sons and daughters to rise up in the spirit of Elijah? We need voices who will speak truth in boldness and who won't back down even when they are speaking to those in positions of power.*

*If we're being honest, we often assume those prophetic voices are men and women somewhere "out there." Someone older and wiser, or who must have a higher calling and more education. Because surely it can't be you.*

*But I came to tell you today that it is you.*

*You're the one who has been called. In your high school. On your team. In your circle of friends. You are the sounding board for the truth of God's Word. You are the one that is supposed to be the light and hope in the midst of the darkness.*

*I'm praying this week that God gives you ears to hear what the Holy Spirit is saying to you. That way you can be His mouthpiece to declare it to everyone who comes across your path.*

# Press Play

*If God said it, let's _____ it (1 Kings 18:41).*

*You don't adapt to your _____. As you live in light of God's _____, your surroundings need to begin to adapt to you, as you communicate God's _____ and His promises clearly.*

*Elijah did not side with the _____.*

# Discuss

*As you sit in the dark room, what significance does a single light have?*

*God calls us to be a light in the darkness. What might that look like for you?*

Okay, if you had the lights off, you can turn them back on now! I wanted you to see that even though one light doesn't seem like much, it does make a difference. And when you stand firm in the promises of God, you will be the light that makes a difference in your school, in your neighborhood, on your team, and in your home.

Even though Elijah didn't have other people standing with him, and even though there was no proof that God would come through, Elijah still chose to trust in the goodness of God. And he still proclaimed that goodness for all to hear.

*What promises of God from His Word do you need to be proclaiming over your circumstances?*

*Who is someone in your life that needs to hear God's truth? How can you be the one to share it?*

Speak God's promises to those who are around you, who are despairing, who are unsettled, who have lost their emotional equilibrium, who are being sucked in to all the discouragement they feel because of what they're facing and what they see happening in the world around us. Be the light in the midst of the darkness.

Listen, the Holy Spirit is the one who will heighten your spiritual senses, who will remind you of God's promises, and then give you clarity on how they apply to your specific circumstances. He will also be the one who gives you the boldness to proclaim those promises to everyone around you.

If God said it, then you be the one to proclaim.

> *Open your Bible and read 1 Kings 18:42. What posture does Elijah take on Carmel? What might that indicate he was doing?*

What does this tell us? It tells us that if God said it, not only should we proclaim it, but we should also pray in alignment with it. Whatever promises God has given you, you should pray toward those promises in alignment with those truths that God has given us.

> *Why should we pray about something that God has already promised to do?*

Prayer is a privilege that God has given us to, in a way, become a partner with Him in his activity being realized on earth. Prayer doesn't manipulate God. It doesn't force His hand. He just allows us to be His partner in the process. Prayer is, as I've said earlier and want to reiterate again, a key that God has given us, so that we can unlock what He plans to do anyway.

*What are you praying about right now? How are you aligning yourselves with God's promises as you pray?*

*Now, let's look at what happens next. Read verse 43.*

"Go up now, look toward the sea."

If God said it, proclaim it. If God said it, then pray in alignment with it. If God said it, I mean, if you really believe God said it, then let's look for it.

There are two beautiful lessons that I see here. The first is that Elijah refused to lead a lazy prayer life. He prioritized prayer. Yes, indeed he did. But he also had his eyes peeled, looking to take notice of what was happening in the atmosphere. He wanted to be aware of when God was actually moving in his circumstances, in his surroundings.

*When have you seen God working in circumstances around you? What might we miss if we aren't watching?*

*Why do we sometimes need others to see how God is moving in our surroundings? How can we encourage one another to look for God's faithfulness in our daily lives?*

The comrade of Elijah's did not downplay even the smallest hint of Yahweh's faithfulness. As soon as that servant caught sight of the beginnings of God's movement, even just a cloud the size of a hand, he reported it to Elijah as encouragement that rain was on the way. We need friends like that. We need people who are going to encourage us about what they do see instead of constantly reminding us of what they don't see. Do you have people like that in your life?

# Press Play

*If God said it, let's _____ _____ for it (1 Kings 18:44).*

*Faith is acting like it _____ _____, even when it's _____ _____, so that it might _____ _____, simply because God _____ _____.*

*Make choices based on where you are headed, not based on _____ _____ _____ right now.*

# Discuss

*How do we prepare for a future that we do not know and cannot see?*

*What are some daily decisions that have lifelong consequences (brushing your teeth, studying for a test, and so on)?*

*How could living out your faith in Christ today impact you 5, 10, and 50 years from now?*

DAY ONE

# Rest Awhile

---

*"Come with me by yourselves to a quiet place
and get some rest."*

**MARK 6:31, NIV**

---

*As we move into 1 Kings 19, identify the following happenings
in Elijah's life from the end of the previous chapter. Start in
1 Kings 18:40.*

- Verse 40: He _____ the prophets of _____.
- Verse 41: He met again with _____.
- Verse 42: He climbed to the top of _____ and he

  _____.
- Verse 43: He sent his servant to look for rain clouds _____

  times.
- Verse 44: He dispatched a follow-up message to

  _____.
- Verse 45: He watched the sky grow _____ with clouds

  and wind.
- Verse 46: He _____ all the way to _____.

While Elijah engaged in all this activity, he told Ahab to refresh himself with food and drink (1 Kings 18:41-42). Between the spiritual battle he'd just been through on Mount Carmel and the physical energy he'd expended in running eighteen miles to Jezreel, the Bible says nothing about Elijah stopping to sleep, eat, or get a drink of water. He simply kept going.

*Turn to Mark 6, a chapter which chronicles an exceptionally
busy season of ministry for Jesus' twelve disciples. Read
verses 7-13, as well as verses 30-31, then come back here to
answer the following questions:*

- What had the disciples been busy doing?

- What had they neglected to do?

- What advice did Jesus give them?

Like the disciples, you'll undoubtedly encounter seasons of life that require more of you than other times, when you need to push yourself past where you think your body can go. But don't convince yourself that by virtue of being a Christian, you are immune from needing to consider your physical needs. Burnout is not a sign of spirituality. That is a fallacy, and it is dangerous. Sooner or later, the neglect will catch up to you.

God knows that we are human. His Spirit lives in us, yes, but we can only be as effective as our physical bodies will allow. It's not unspiritual to tend to our physical, emotional, and mental needs. And in one of my favorite portions of Elijah's narrative, Yahweh's response to the prophet is about to show us that. First, however, let's learn from a couple of counterproductive things Elijah did that enhanced his compromised condition.

## 1. ALL BY MYSELF

"[He] came to Beersheba, which belongs to Judah; and he left his servant there."

**1 KINGS 19:3b**

*What did Elijah do when he got there?*

One of the enemy's driving motivations is to bring division within the body of Christ—to isolate whole groups of us from others for illegitimate reasons, or to cause brokenness in healthy relationships where caring support would otherwise occur. Unity among brothers and sisters in Christ forms a firm line of defense against Satan's advances, and he knows it. That's why he works against it.

So when you're in a place in life where you're feeling completely worn out, one of his leading lies will encourage you to overinflate your belief that there's no one else who can understand what you're facing. *No one. You're on your own now, buddy.* That's exactly where we find Elijah in 1 Kings 19. His despair had distorted his perspective until he felt he was "the only one left" (v. 14, NIV) who was devoted to God.

*According to 1 Kings 19:18, what was the truth?*

*Read forward to verses 19-21. What did he gain that further discredited his self-pitying perspective?*

*How do you find this same distorted perspective taking shape in your own thinking when you're discouraged, tired, or overwhelmed?*

> "Two are better than one because they have a good return for their efforts. For if either falls, his companion can lift him up; but pity to the one who falls without another to lift him up. Also, if two lie down together, they can keep warm; but how can one person alone keep warm? And if someone overpowers one person, two can resist him. A cord of three strands is not easily broken."
>
> **ECCLESIASTES 4:9-12**

*Read the passage from Ecclesiastes 4 in the margin. Write down any observations you make from it. Prayerfully consider if a fractured friendship or relationship in your life reveals the enemy's handiwork in separating you from needed reinforcement (and separating them from yours).*

*Write down something practical you can do today to counteract the enemy's goal and retain this relationship (if possible)?*

If you're participating in this study with a group, the girls around you are partners in this season of your journey. They are part of what God has given you to offer encouragement, strength, realignment, restoration, and so much more. While adding unhealthy or unnecessary relationships to your life is not beneficial during difficult seasons of life, neither is pushing away godly friendships that hold you accountable and help facilitate emotional stability. Learn a hard lesson from Elijah: *Don't isolate.*

## 2. MISPLACED EXPECTATIONS

Elijah had honored Yahweh's instructions to the best of his ability at every step of the way. And yet he appears to have done so with unspoken, maybe even subconscious expectations about what the end results would be.

He'd understandably hoped that his actions would precipitate an immediate national revival, the kind where people in every crevice of the Israelite community, from the top rungs of government on down, would pledge their complete allegiance to the one true God. Initially, that's what the people had *said* on Mount Carmel.

But the king had feasted and not repented, and Jezebel was still on her rampage. Things just hadn't panned out the way Elijah had expected. And the disappointment was killing him.

*Focus in on Elijah's final comment in verse 4.*
*What comparison was he making?*

For Elijah, this season of fatigue uncovered an inflated ego underneath his tough exterior. Apparently some of his devastation extended from not doing better than his forefathers—from not quickly and completely leading Israel back to God. He thought his ministry would be different. Better than theirs. The first of its kind. But comparison and misplaced expectations had derailed his emotional stability. He was pummeled with self-condemnation, disappointment, and regret about his failure to achieve something that God never even expected of him.

> *"He went on a day's journey into the wilderness. He sat down under a broom tree and prayed that he might die. He said, 'I have had enough! LORD, take my life, for I'm no better than my ancestors.'"*
>
> **1 KINGS 19:4, CSB**

And now, in this critical moment of the prophet's life—when he was the most depleted, vulnerable, fatigued, depressed, and disillusioned—Yahweh stepped in with practical nourishment. He didn't rebuke him, nor did he ignore or discard him. Instead, watch with me as He refreshes him with the most basic of human needs.

*After reading 1 Kings 19:5-9, spend your last few minutes of time today with these questions:*

*What did God allow Elijah to do?*

*What did He make provision for Elijah to have?*



*What does this reveal about how Yahweh viewed His prophet?*



*How does Yahweh's response to Elijah in the Old Testament mirror Jesus' response to the disciples in the New Testament?*



*How does His reaction to Elijah give you a sense of freedom regarding your own limitations and humanity?*



With as many profound principles as we've gleaned from Elijah's narrative over the past six weeks, I wouldn't be surprised if this one is the most liberating you've experienced thus far. God is not mad at you because your body is tired or your mind is frayed or your soul is unusually heavy—not after the kind of project you've just finished, or the difficulties you've just endured, or the emotional marathon you've just run. He isn't agitated by the limitations of your flesh. Instead, He stands patiently ready to minister to you, to work through those deficiencies, and to nourish you as you recover from them.

With all the busyness, legalism, strictness, and tension that may be an ongoing part of your daily life, take a moment to breathe deeply, enjoying the gracious and sincere affection of your Father today. He sees. He knows.

> "He restores my soul."
>
> **PSALM 23:3**

Sister, rest.

And while you're at it, "Eat, because the journey is too great for you" (v. 7, NKJV).

Nothing unspiritual about that.

## DAY TWO

# Off Message

*"Jezebel sent a messenger to Elijah."*

### 1 KINGS 19:2

Elijah's journey up to this point has been punctuated by one extreme scenario after another. When you take into account the cumulative effects of what he'd faced during his ministry, he had truly been operating on bionic-level doses of adrenaline for several years. It's understandable, then, that the next chapter would begin to chronicle his crash. And in a way, I'm grateful that it does. Because it reminds us that *everyone*—even mighty representatives of God who are on mission and fulfilling their divine assignments—are still human and in need of safeguarding.

But today I want you to see how Elijah's natural vulnerability intersected with something—with *someone*—that pushed him over the edge.

*Read 1 Kings 19:1-3. What does this passage indicate as the tipping point that brought on Elijah's meltdown?*

*"And he was afraid, and got up and ran for his life and came to Beersheba, which belongs to Judah; and left his servant there."*

**1 KINGS 19:3**

*Underline the descriptive phrases from verse 3 that reveal his emotional response and the actions it led to. Below, add any depth about what Elijah's actions reveal.*

In only a few short verses, the same man who "outran Ahab" into town after the arrival of a rainstorm (1 Kings 18:46) has turned into a man who "ran for his life." Despite the Lord's hand still being on him—which it is—there's certainly a marked difference in this version of God's prophet. The bold, fearless, prayer-warrior prophet of God has become fragile, insecure, and depressed. The question is: *Why?*

> "Even mighty representatives of God who are on mission and fulfilling their divine assignments are still human and in need of safeguarding."
>
> **#ELIJAHBIBLESTUDY**

Answer: Because in this moment of understandable exhaustion and emotional depletion, his primary enemy had sent him a message. And not only did the message get through to him, but …

He believed it.

> *Read 1 Kings 19:2 again. Write out Jezebel's threat to Elijah word-for-word in the space below.*

> *Take a look at 2 Kings 2:10-11, which chronicles Elijah's last moments on Earth. What light does this shed on the veracity of Jezebel's threat?*

Jezebel's contempt for Elijah had been boiling for a long time. She already despised him for his bold stance on the side of Yahweh during three contentious, continuous years without rain. She was even more furious now at how he'd embarrassed her beloved prophets of Baal in the showdown on Mount Carmel—the same prophets she'd invested her time and personal finances to support. And when her weak, spineless husband came whining to her about how Elijah had seized and slaughtered those same defeated prophets in the Kishon Valley, her fury soared off the charts.

Elijah was going to pay. Elijah must suffer.

> "Brace yourself against the enemy's message."
>
> #ELIJAHBIBLESTUDY

Please notice that she didn't send a hit man. She didn't rally a squadron of mercenaries to surround him. She *could* have done those things, because she obviously knew his location. But it's clear that she wasn't as interested in delivering the edge of a sword as she was in delivering a carefully worded message. Instead of going to the trouble of killing him, she knew that the *threat* of death would be a worse punishment than death itself. She didn't need to kill Elijah if she could demoralize, discourage, and derail him enough to want to kill himself. And as much as I hate to say it, she was right.

*What did Elijah pray for in 1 Kings 19:4?*

Jezebel's tactics are actually an Old Testament example of a New Testament principle and warning—a demonic ploy still used against the people of God to this day. The devil is our enemy, our "adversary." He is hoping that the lies he suggests and the methods of discouragement he employs will lead God's people to despondency and hopelessness.

As Christians, we cannot be destroyed. Our eternal destiny is secured. But if we are not on guard, proactively rehearsing and renewing our minds with God's promises, the enemy's threats will take root and blossom into full-blown despair. Especially in seasons of vulnerability.

> *Your adversary, the devil, prowls around like a roaring lion, seeking someone to devour."*
>
> **1 PETER 5:8**

Such was the case with Elijah. Despite the victory and fortitude he exhibited on Carmel, his fragility proved a perfect breeding ground for Jezebel's lie. With the door opened after his adrenaline crash, her message had all the nutrients it needed in order to take root, fester, and mushroom out of control. This way, he'd turn into a fear-ridden fugitive running away into the wilderness. He'd be robbed of the confidence, peace, and vision for remaining effective as a prophet. He'd be eaten up with too much anxiety and apprehension to get back in the fray again.

If her message could make him afraid enough, he'd forget what God had already done. In Cherith. In Zarephath. On Carmel. And the prophet would stop trusting Him with the future.

*The devil is constantly "prowling," assuming a posture that is menacing and threatening. He is hunting with intention to kill—"seeking" to devour, though not actually doing it.*

During the times when you are weakened, whether physically or emotionally, you must be intentional about girding yourself against the enemy's schemes. Put on the full armor of God and be vigilant about it. Make sure that you are fitted securely with the helmet of salvation so that your mind remains protected against his lies and attempts to take advantage of you. When you sense thoughts and ideas bombarding your mind that are contrary to how the Bible defines your identity in Christ and His nature toward you—especially after a season of success OR a period of extreme difficulty and hardship—prepare in advance to immediately discard the devil's deceptions. He is hoping you'll let down your guard in times of exhaustion, so you'll believe his lies and threats over the truths of God.

Remember this:

> "The weapons of our warfare are not of the flesh, but divinely powerful for the destruction of fortresses. We are destroying arguments and all arrogance raised against the knowledge of God, and we are taking every thought captive to the obedience of Christ."

**2 CORINTHIANS 10:4-5**

You don't have to cave to his threats. You can be strong, even when you're weak. Fortify yourself in specific, strategic prayer. Arm yourself with specific promises from God's Word, asking His Spirit to guide you to places in His Word that directly refute the enemy's messaging. Consistently rehearse what God has already done on your behalf.

Defeat the message, and you'll defeat the messenger.

# DAY THREE
# Location Services

*"Then he came there to a cave and spent the night there; and behold, the word of the LORD came to him."*

**1 KINGS 19:9**

One of the most meaningful aspects of our redemption in Christ is that you and I can never reach a place so far away that we're beyond the reach of our Father's love, grace, and mercy. This gospel truth brings tears to my eyes when I contemplate the fact that He can reach me wherever I am, no matter how bleak or dry the wilderness I'm traveling through.

David captured it well when he said,

> Where can I go from Your Spirit? Or where can I flee from Your presence? If I ascend to heaven, You are there; If I make my bed in Sheol, behold, You are there. ... If I say, "Surely the darkness will overwhelm me, and the light around me will be night," even the darkness is not dark to You, and the night is as bright as the day. Darkness and light are alike to You.

**PSALM 139:7-8,11-12**

So whether I choose a far road of my own volition, or whether I'm pressed into it by circumstances outside my control, either way He is somehow able to make *every* road, even the most difficult road, lead back toward Him.

When I look back on the seasons of my life when I felt the most distant, I now see that even my best efforts at hiding were not effective in keeping me from Him. He still came to find me.

To reclaim me.

To draw me back to Himself.

This is true for all of us. Just like it was true for Elijah.

***Read the following verses and underline the spot where Elijah's journey led him after forty days of traveling through the wilderness.***

He arose and ate and drank, and he journeyed in the strength of that food for forty days and forty nights to Horeb, the mountain of God. Then he came there to a cave and spent the night there.

**1 KINGS 19:8-9a**

*Mount Horeb is the same as Mount Sinai, which is where Moses received the Ten Commandments.*

Elijah's depression had grown so severe that he willingly launched himself into the vast, barren desert, six long weeks away from his last known stop. The location where he ended up was far south of where the rest of his travels had taken place. He couldn't have known at this point if he'd ever see another human being again or if he'd be able to survive the return trip, should he decide to head back.

This season of his solitude is distinct from his time at Cherith, the dwindling brook where God specifically sent him and promised to provide for him. Fear and despondency have been the only guides leading him into this desert, dictating his direction and actions. Clearly the tone of this portion of Elijah's story is a complete departure from the focused, purpose-filled journey thus far.

*The Hebrew text reveals that Elijah went to "THE" ← CAVE—presumably a reference to the cave of Moses.[1]*

And yet, God's redemptive purposes were still alive down here in the wilderness. This uncharted road will lead Elijah to an encounter with God that will reinvigorate, redirect, and refocus him. Here on this mountain, and here in this cave, he'll discover he can still hear God's voice and he can still participate in God's plan, despite the discouraged doubts that his effectiveness had come to a disparaging end. Yahweh can make sure that even a trip through the Sinai Desert will not have been in vain.

I'm so glad this segment of Elijah's story is included in Scripture, aren't you? It reminds me that God is there—ready and waiting for us—even when circumstances have redirected us or we have foolishly run into a wilderness of our own. In reality, this redemptive thread is what the Bible is all about, which is why evidences of it are scattered all over Scripture.

Choose two of the following biblical personalities for a short case study. Read the passage for each, and then answer the following questions in the space provided:

- Hagar (Gen. 16:1-13)
- Jacob (Gen. 27:42-45; 28:10-22)
- Moses (Ex. 3:1-12)
- Gideon (Judg. 6:11-24; 7:16-21)
- Peter (Luke 22:54-62; Acts 2:32-36)
- Paul (2 Cor. 1:5-11)

- How would you describe their emotional state? Which words or phrases led you to this conclusion?
- What setting or circumstances were they enduring that might have made them feel hopeless, despairing, and distant from God?
- How did they experience God and His character in a uniquely personal way?
- How did the person's life change as a result of this encounter?
- Of the two people you studied, which one did you most relate to? What elements of their story seem the most familiar to you, and why?

*How do you see God present in your life right now, and how is He turning your current wilderness into a highway toward Him? Below, record how you're sensing that He is redirecting you, changing you, revealing Himself to you, and repositioning you for something new.*

My forty-fifth birthday was on December 31, 2019. My mother died in my arms the day before. I remember waking up on my birthday in a fog, not even remembering what date it was. To tell you the truth, the numb feeling continued for many months afterward. Unable to delay my own pending surgery, which I told you about, I was immediately thrust into a recovery process of another sort—my body's physical recovery, traveling directly alongside my soul's emotional recovery.

It was tough. On many fronts. I noticed, for example, that I had a hard time digesting new information. Or being mentally productive. Or fully engaging in the most regular and basic of life tasks, as well as staying focused on projects and endeavors that were once enjoyable activities. All the losses we'd endured in recent months had been difficult, but losing my own Mommy? It seemed to push me over the emotional edge. Overnight I felt as though I'd been thrust into a stagnant wilderness of exhaustion and numbness. And admittedly, like Elijah, I journeyed more deeply into it.

That's why this section in Elijah's story—along with that of Hagar and Jacob, Moses and Gideon, Peter and Paul, and a whole bunch of others—has really encouraged me. Their examples remind me that even when my paths are hurtful, disappointing, earth-shattering, or unexplainable, those same paths can still put me in prime position to experience God in a new way. To see Him from a new vantage point. To relate to Him and understand Him in a different, more mature, more dynamic way for the future.

The hound of heaven can find us no matter where we are.

> "Am I a God at hand, declares the LORD, and not a God far away? Can a man hide himself in secret places so that I cannot see him? declares the LORD. Do I not fill heaven and earth? declares the LORD."
>
> **JEREMIAH 23:23-24, ESV**

Mount Horeb is in this desert, sis. And even here we'll find God waiting for us. Nothing we're walking through has the power to take us away from Him. Instead, inexplicably, we'll be drawn closer to Him. All the pain or sadness or disappointment we may feel in these difficult places won't disappear, but the hope of His presence will break our fall.

It puts the brakes on despair. His presence is like a bungee cord that yanks us back from the perilous death spiral of utter hopelessness.

Be encouraged and know that even this road—the one that goes off the map—is a road that can lead you back to Him. I know it doesn't seem so, but because of His redemptive grace, you're actually headed in a direction brimming with the beauty and brilliance of a divine encounter. This road leads to the mountain of God.

And He is already there ahead of you.

**Pray this:**

*Father, I am dry and lonely. I am tired and out of answers. I don't see how I'll ever get beyond this and feel right again about anything. But even though I do feel lost and rudderless right now, I believe—by faith—that You haven't lost **me**. Thank You for being willing AND able to make this wilderness my next step in a new direction. You will lead me through it and meet me on the other side. In Jesus' name, amen.*

# What Are You Doing Here?

*"[Elijah] came there to a cave and spent the night there; and behold, the word of the LORD came to him, and He said to him, 'What are you doing here, Elijah?'"*

**1 KINGS 19:9**

God is good at asking questions. And whenever He does, we can be sure He already knows the answer. Divine inquiries are never for our Father's benefit; He poses them with the intention of helping us see the truth of our situation, be honest with ourselves, and then agree with Him about His solution for us. God's questions require an authentic soul-searching to help us exhume issues of the heart that we hadn't formerly recognized or have been choosing to ignore. They make us dig deeply, beyond the surface layer of hurt and disappointment, past the veneer of happiness we've cleverly placed before others. By the time we've dealt with a question from God, He has shown us where we *really* are, and He has placed on the doorstep of our lives the next opportunity for us to mature in our faith and experience His power.

**FOR GROUP DISCUSSION:**
*Why do you think God may have asked Elijah two identical questions—first when Elijah came* **into** *the cave, and next when he was coming out of it?*

*Look at 1 Kings 19:9, as well as verse 13. Write down the identical question that Yahweh asked Elijah.*

*Ask the Holy Spirit how this question applies to you right now in your life—spiritually, emotionally, and relationally. Before you fully launch into this lesson, invite Him to pierce through any superficial layers of denial or deflection you've erected, and to show you the particular truths He wants you to recognize about where you* really *are in any specific area and what got you there. Record below anything He brings to mind.*

For Elijah, Yahweh's question wasn't as much about addressing his geographical location; it was about the internal spiritual state that had driven him there. This holy question unearthed deep-seated realities that Elijah needed to address, and it cleared the way for his attention to be refocused, his hearing to be refined, and his path to be redirected.

As this scene unfolds in 1 Kings 19, it begins with a question designed to shift Elijah's perspective on himself and his prophetic ministry.

**Take the time to read and savor this entire event in Elijah's life (1 Kings 19:11-21). We'll refer back to it throughout the remainder of today's lesson, as well as tomorrow, so keep your Bible nearby. After you finish reading, meet me back here.**

**Zero in on verse 11 and compare it with verse 10 in the margin, paying close attention to the highlighted portions. How does the main focus shift between the two verses? What is their noticeable difference in tone and emphasis?**

**Now compare Elijah's response to the question in verse 10 with his response to the same question in verse 14. What insight does this discovery give you regarding how stubbornly embedded our self-deception can be?**

God's question, in conjunction with the remarkable happenings soon to follow, are about to expose a mound of self-focused pity that had consumed Elijah's thinking. Yahweh's voice not only beckoned Elijah to come out of the dank, dark cave where he'd run and hidden himself away—not only to come out of there *physically*—but also to emerge spiritually, mentally, and emotionally from the self-obsession he'd allowed to overtake his whole outlook on life. All at once, with one pinpointed question, God was commanding His prophet to readjust his position and his focus, to walk out of the darkness in all regards, so that his vision could be set once again on the Lord.

> He [Elijah] replied, "I have been very zealous for the LORD God of Armies, but the Israelites have abandoned your covenant, torn down your altars, and killed your prophets with the sword. I alone am left, and they are looking for me to take my life." Then [God] said, "Go out and stand on the mountain in the Lord's presence." At that moment, the Lord passed by. A great and mighty wind was tearing at the mountains and was shattering cliffs before the Lord, but the Lord was not in the wind. After the wind there was an earthquake, but the Lord was not in the earthquake.
>
> **1 KINGS 19:10-11, CSB**

We can attest, having spent six weeks in detailed study on the happenings that took place at Cherith, Zarephath, and Carmel, as well as the intensely personal interactions they necessitated, that Elijah's life had been marked by being consistently preoccupied with Yahweh's presence and purpose. Despite many earlier opportunities to exert a me-first, self-willed reaction toward God's challenging, uncomfortable demands, Elijah proved unshakable. His commitment to prayer carried him through the many difficult days and even more lonesome nights. His fixed focus on Yahweh kept him upright, kept him moving, or at times kept him sitting perfectly still, for whatever the word of the Lord called him to do at any given moment. His attention was always true north, single-minded, laser-focused on surrendering all personal rights and preferences to the greater good of God's plans for divine renewal. Whatever it cost.

But now, here at Horeb, things were different. With his spiritual gaze and eyesight lowered from heaven down to earth, with his emotions misdirected onto himself and his circumstances, Elijah had become a shell of whom he once was. Faith had taken a back seat to fear. Hope had been overshadowed by hopelessness. Expectancy had succumbed to dread.

### ELIJAH, WHAT ARE YOU DOING *HERE*?
### HOW DID YOU GET *HERE*?

This is, in fact, the only outcome where the road of unrestrained introspection ever leads. The trajectory of a heart that's turned inwardly on itself cannot help but take a downward path. Becoming obsessed with ourselves is sure to lead toward a dramatic pitfall into fear and insecurity.

Take the example of Peter, for instance, when he saw Jesus walking on the water:

> Peter responded and said to Him, "Lord, if it is You, command me to come to You on the water." And He said, "Come!" And Peter got out of the boat and walked on the water, and came toward Jesus. But seeing the wind, he became frightened, and when he began to sink, he cried out, saying, "Lord, save me!"

**MATTHEW 14:28-30**

A misplaced focus, an overly sensitive concern with self or circumstances, changes everything. And it will consistently beg a question of God—even as it brought an attentive question from Jesus to Peter, as He "reached out with His hand and took hold of him, and said to him, 'You of little faith, why did you doubt?'" (v. 31).

Questions are simply God's way of reminding you to fix your eyes back on Him.

So, really, *what are you doing here?*

The Lord was there on the mountain with Elijah, and He is here today, too, to open us up to His revelation of truth—the truth about Him, about ourselves, about our circumstances, about everything. He has come to ask the kinds of questions that will draw us out of fear and self-pity so that we can "go out and stand on the mountain" (1 Kings 19:11a) with a willingness to let God take us wherever He wants us to go.

> *Having come prayerfully to the end of today's lesson, talk to the Lord about what He wants to shift in you as a result of the answers that His questions are unearthing. Confess any ways that you've been overly focused on yourself or your circumstances. And now fix your eyes back on Him. Ask the Holy Spirit to help you throughout the next twenty-four hours to continually adjust your attention so that it is squarely situated on Jesus.*

# Earth, Wind, and Fire

---

*"Behold, the LORD was passing by!"*

**1 KINGS 19:11b**

---

We arrive now at this culminating message from Elijah's encounter with Yahweh on Mount Sinai, also known as Horeb. It comes with heartfelt encouragement, but also with a course correction against this tendency for trying to make the work of God formulaic and predictable. I hope we'll emerge stirred with holy anticipation for what God has prepared for our lives in the weeks, months, and years to come.

> *Yesterday you read 1 Kings 19:11-21 in its entirety. Reread just the portion printed below, zeroing in on the various elements of nature that Elijah encountered on the mountain. Circle each one.*

[God] said, "Go out and stand on the mountain before the LORD." And behold, the LORD was passing by! And a great and powerful wind was tearing out the mountains and breaking the rocks in pieces before the LORD; but the LORD was not in the wind. And after the wind there was an earthquake, but the LORD was not in the earthquake. And after the earthquake, a fire, but the LORD was not in the fire; and after the fire, a sound of a gentle blowing. When Elijah heard it, he wrapped his face in his cloak and went out and stood in the entrance of the cave."

**1 KINGS 19:11-13a**

Record the progression of Elijah's experience. The Lord was *not* in ...

1.
2.
3.

Beloved sister, as you walk forward in your journey with the Lord, remember that His presence is not always characterized as something that thrills us—an emotional reaction that startles us; a big, bold event that awakens us; a flashy circumstance that wows us; or a miraculous, eye-opening occurrence that surprises us. Just because it's extraordinary—just because it's cut from the earthquake, hurricane, or wildfire variety—doesn't mean it's automatically Him at work. Just because it's hyper doesn't mean it's holy. This misconception will inevitably blind us to the occasions when His authentic activity is in the "sound of a gentle blowing."

> Look at the beautiful ways that Elijah's experience with God on Mount Sinai is rendered in different translations
> of the passage:
> * "A low whisper" (ESV)
> * "Sheer silence" (NRSV)
> * "A gentle blowing" (NASB)
> * "A still small voice" (KJV)
> * "A soft whisper" (CSB)

> *How did Elijah respond when he heard it (v. 13)?*

The contrast between the earthquake, the tumultuous wind, the searing fire, and the hushed, holy whisper of God is striking. The first three were loud and attention-getting; the last one was nearly imperceptible. But the contrast is symbolic of what God appeared to be doing in His continued work with the nation of Israel. As the stormy, volatile ministry of Elijah moved toward its conclusion, the relatively gentle ministry of his protégé, Elisha, was soon to dawn.

It was time for a stiller, smaller voice.

Detecting God's presence in these quieter ways requires patience and a keen spiritual ear, the kind He's been developing in you throughout every day of our Bible study together. And this sensitivity will continue to develop in you as you keep walking with Him and growing in grace. His voice will draw you out of the caves of despair, disillusionment, and discouragement and will usher you into a freedom and newfound reverence for Him, a renewed and hopeful outlook for the future—based on the certainty of His Word.

The stillness of God's manifest presence drew Elijah to his feet. He wrapped his cloak over his face in reverence, and he came out to stand at the mouth of the cave. Then God spoke to him, giving him a new assignment and role in His divine purposes for the future.

**Turn to 1 Kings 19:15-16. Wade through all the names there and boil it down to the three major directives that Yahweh gave Elijah.**

1. Anoint _____ as king over Aram.
2. Anoint _____ as king over Israel.
3. Anoint _____ as prophet.

The beautiful lesson surging underneath this moment in Elijah's life—hearing the Lord speak to him in the "sheer silence"—is that God beckoned him to a new calling and method of ministry. This means Elijah's despondency had not disqualified him from being a key player in the goal of calling Israel back to allegiance to Yahweh. He was still a part of God's purpose, and, hallelujah, so are you!

So am I!

National revival had always been Elijah's divinely assigned objective, but the prophet had been pursuing this goal from one specific angle—the one in which his efforts alone accomplished the goal. He'd been obedient in his actions, but his presumption became the direct catalyst for his deep discouragement. He felt like he'd failed.

But now, God speaks again, here on Mount Horeb, clarifying to Elijah that despite his disappointment, he still has a key role to play. He was to anoint a specific new king over Aram (also known as Syria), as well as a specific new king over Israel, and was also to formally pass the baton to a new man who would carry on the prophetic mantle that Elijah had carried so diligently and faithfully. The combined efforts of these individuals would be strategic in bringing Ahab and Jezebel's rule to a sure end and spurring Israel toward the unhindered worship of Yahweh that they'd been redeemed to enjoy.

God's work would still be done; it just wouldn't all be done by Elijah. His prophetic assignment was not yet over, but it was now time—in God's time— for his ministry to be redirected. In this wilderness, and in that still small voice, God was telling Elijah that he continued to be significant to the Lord's divine purposes.

Sister, you are still significant to the fulfillment of God's plan. No matter your age or demographic, your temperament, or your previous disappointments, you are a necessary part of what He's advancing and accomplishing on the earth. There is nothing (and I do mean *nothing!*) that has rendered you useless or expendable to Him. Don't let your expectations about how your part is supposed to look or how God will reveal it to you discourage you from being yielded and available for what He is asking you to do right now.

Shhhhh. Listen.

The Lord is passing by.

This, too, is the legacy of Elijah. Not just fire, not just Mount Carmel. The legacy of Elijah includes this much-needed reminder that less-flashy work is no less God's work. And that the later days of one's life and ministry can still be fruitful, effective, important, valuable parts of what God wants done in this generation. Not only can be, but *need* to be.

Elijah's story is God's story, just as your story and my story are God's story. The process He takes us through, as well as the pinnacles He takes us to, show us He doesn't want us left out of the mission He's working to accomplish. There is always something next, something here, something *now* that He's been preparing you to do—through the growing times, through the waiting times, through the up times, even through the down times. These are *our* times—this is *your* time.

He's whispering to you even now, giving you new direction, new insight, and fresh encouragement. He's reminding you that He still has a divine plan with generational implications, and this plan involves *you*—running full speed ahead, even if it takes you down a path you weren't anticipating, and then passing the baton of faith along to others who will run alongside you, as well as beyond you.

Modern-day Elijah, be faithful.

Don't give up.

There's work to be done.

You are still significant to the fulfillment of God's plan.

#ELIJAHBIBLESTUDY

# Heavenward

## FAITH, FAILURE, AND BEYOND

 **Fire:** Submitting to God's Power

# Press Play

God knew all these things, _____ them all in, and still _____ us to be

_____ for His _____.

Every time we see their failures, it should underscore the fact that we are looking for a

_____, that we need somebody else to be our _____.

Jesus has _____ been and will always be the _____, the _____, and

the _____.

# Discuss

*Looking back over the past six sessions, which part of Elijah's story do you relate to the most? Why?*

*If someone were to tell you, "God isn't done with you yet," what would you say?*

FOR

# Leaders & Moms

# Hey Leader!

I am so glad you decided to lead this study through the story of Elijah! I hope these tips and instructions will allow you to lead your group of girls in the most effective and God-honoring way.

### Pray diligently.

Ask God to prepare you to lead this study. Pray individually and specifically for the girls in your group. Make this a priority in your personal walk and preparation.

### Prepare adequately.

Don't just wing this. Take time to preview each session so you have a good grasp of the content. Look over the group session and consider your girls. Feel free to delete, reword, or add questions that fit your group better.

### Provide resources.

Each student will need a Bible study book. Try to have extras on hand for girls who join the group later in the study. Also suggest girls bring a Bible and journal to group each week.

### Encourage freely.

Cheer for your girls and encourage them to participate in every part of the study.

### Lead by example.

Make sure you complete all of the personal study. Be willing to share your story, what you're learning, and your questions with your group.

### Be aware.

If girls are hesitant to discuss their thoughts and questions in a large group, consider a small group setting more conducive to conversation.

### Follow up.

If a student mentions a prayer request or need, make sure to follow up. It may be a situation where the group can get involved in helping out.

### Evaluate often.

After each session, assess what needs to be changed to more effectively lead the study.

## LET'S TALK.

Each session has been designed with a Let's Talk section to help you lead your girls through a fun, engaging, yet deep discussion of the story of Elijah found in Scripture. Below you will find what you can expect to do each time you and your girls meet.

## WELCOME.

Prepare ahead of time to let the girls engage with one other at the beginning of each group time. Before you jump into the video and discussion for the day, take some time to let the girls share about their personal study from the previous session then break the ice with a fun starter activity. We've listed some ideas on the next few pages under the correlating sessions.

## PRESS PLAY.

There is a teaching video that goes along with each session of the Bible study. You will "Press Play" twice during your time together. Before you watch the video, encourage the girls to take notes and fill in the blanks as they watch. You can find the answers to those blanks on the following pages. The videos are available for purchase and rent at lifeway.com/elijah.

## PAUSE.

Keep the remote close by as you watch each session's video. You will be hitting pause during the teaching to help you stop to engage in discussion with your girls before watching the remainder of the video. Check out the fun (yet optional) PAUSE activities ahead of time listed on the next few pages.

## DISCUSS.

The Scripture references and questions are provided for you to lead a meaningful discussion with your girls. If you don't get through all of the questions, don't stress. Your goal is to help them get beyond surface-level answers, explore the truth of God's Word, and discover how they can apply it personally.

For FREE shareable art to use as a promotion or for your girls to share with their friends, scan this QR code!

## SESSION 1

**LET'S BEGIN:** Since it's your first week together, plan a few icebreaker activities to do with the girls. Here's one idea: We'll be talking a lot about fire during this study, so to "cool things down" as you begin, give each girl an ice cube to hold in her hand. Afterward, begin asking "get to know you" questions (like "what's your favorite ice cream flavor" or "what sport do you like the most?") to the girls to answer while they attempt to melt the ice in their hands. First girl to melt her ice during the question time, wins!

**PRESS PLAY:** Here are the answers for the fill in the blanks: *Carmel, glory process, process, willing, what Elijah did, what Elijah got*

**PAUSE & DISCUSS:** Before moving into your Discuss section, your girls will high five someone in your group and tell them "It's a process!"

**PRESS PLAY:** Here are the answers for the fill in the blanks: *lives, word, rebellion, power, spirit*

**PRAY:** Close out the session by praying over the girls in your group. Ask the Lord to give them the courage to be His mouthpiece this week.

## SESSION 2

**LET'S BEGIN:** If you read the Intro letter ahead of time, you'll see that Priscilla gives an illustration involving cookies that looked more like pancakes. Offer the girls two batches of cookies: 1) a batch that forgot the flour and 2) a batch of cookies made correctly. Encourage the girls that when we depend on Jesus rather than ourselves, we look more like the yummy batch of cookies rather than the pancake kind.

**PRESS PLAY:** Here are the answers for the fill in the blanks: *separate, prepare, release, go away, reposition, blessings, willing, empowered*

**PAUSE & DISCUSS:** Before moving into your Discuss section, have your girls switch up positions where everyone is currently seated.

**PRESS PLAY:** Here are the answers for the fill in the blanks: *surprise, ask, think, shield, separation, shielded*

**PRAY:** Ask for a volunteer to pray for protection over the other girls as they obey the calling God has placed on their lives.

## SESSION 3

**LET'S BEGIN:** We'll be talking about fear during this session. Ask girls to share what are some physical things they are afraid of in this world: spiders, snakes, tornadoes. Then ask them what their biggest fear in following Jesus might be.

**PRESS PLAY:** Here are the answers for the fill in the blanks: *refined, purified, prepared, uncomfortable, our, their, uncharted, redemption*

**PAUSE & DISCUSS:** Before moving into your Discuss section, grab a small bowl of flour and a little jar of oil to place in the center of your group.

**PRESS PLAY:** Here are the answers for the fill in the blanks: *job, work, foundation, fire*

**PRAY:** Pray over your girls that the Lord would remove any ounce of fear that is keeping them from being bold for Him and putting action behind their faith.

## SESSION 4

**LET'S BEGIN:** Start off with a game. You'll just need a ball (the size and type is dependent upon your space and preference). Have the girls form a circle then pass the ball to each other. However, they can't pass it to the person next to them and they can't pass it to someone who has already caught it. See how fast they can pass it without dropping it!

**PRESS PLAY:** Here are the answers for the fill in the blanks: *bridge, Obadiah, trustworthy, well-respected, good, job, faithful, believer, treasures, earth*

**PAUSE & DISCUSS:** Before moving into your Discuss section, find a ball to pass around as you work through the questions.

**PRESS PLAY:** Here are the answers for the fill in the blanks: *actively, preserving, truths, mundane assignment, divine destiny*

**PRAY:** Ask for a volunteer to pray for the group of girls that they may have eyes to see how God is divinely working in their ordinary circumstances.

## SESSION 5

**LET'S BEGIN:** Play the worship song mentioned in the intro of this session. Encourage your girls to sing along if they feel comfortable!

**PRESS PLAY:** Here are the answers for the fill in the blanks: *fire, in, on*

**PAUSE & DISCUSS:** Before moving into your Discuss section, encourage your girls to find someone in the group and tell them "God ignites the fire."

**PRESS PLAY:** Here are the answers for the fill in the blanks: *underestimate, simple prayer, manipulate, unlocks, planned, opened up, rained, fire*

**PRAY:** Encourage girls to get alone with the Lord for a few minutes about the things they've discussed. Maybe that means kneeling at their seat or spreading out across the home or room. Encourage girls to be honest with the Lord about where they're at and how they might need to repent.

## SESSION 6

**LET'S BEGIN:** Start off with a game of telephone. Ask the girls to form a circle then whisper the title of the session "Do You Hear What I Hear?" into one girl's ear. She then must repeat what she heard to the next girl. No one is allowed to repeat the phrase. See what the last girl of the circle thinks the message is at the end.

**PRESS PLAY:** Here are the answers for the fill in the blanks: *proclaim, surroundings, promises, Word, majority*

**PAUSE & DISCUSS:** Before moving into your Discuss section, turn off all the lights except a single cell phone light. Using the single light, take a few minutes to read and answer the questions. Don't worry, you'll get to turn the lights back on.

**PRESS PLAY:** Here are the answers for the fill in the blanks: *actively prepare, is so, not so, be so, said so, where you are*

**PRAY:** Pray over the girls in your group that they may see the future the Lord is building for them. Ask Him to sustain them as they daily walk in obedience of Him.

## SESSION 7

**LET'S BEGIN:** This is your last week together, so the video and discussion time will be shorter. This gives you more time to celebrate all that you and your girls accomplished through your study together. Make it special by having food or fun games, and maybe even assemble a bonfire for the girls to enjoy. Because nothing says Elijah, like a good fire.

**PRESS PLAY:** Here are the answers for the fill in the blanks: *factored, allows, utilized, purposes, Messiah, Savior, always,*

**PRAY:** Pray and thank the Lord for all He has done in the lives of your girls. Ask Him to equip them and protect them as they follow after Him and live out their faith in a dark and broken world.

# Hey Mom!

We are so excited that you have decided to complete this study with your daughter!

Priscilla Shirer's study through the story of Elijah will not only challenge and embolden your personal faith in Him, but we hope that you will see transformation take place in your daughter as she rises to her calling.

## For This Study You Will Need:

• Elijah: *Women's Bible Study Book* for yourself

• Elijah: *Teen Girl Bible Study Book* for your daughter(s)

• Elijah: Video Sessions (purchase or rent)

## How To Utilize Your Materials Together:

### WATCH
• Watch the weekly video with your daughter.

• Utilize the questions found under Discuss of each week's Let's Talk section located in the teen girl Bible study book.

*A note about the video content:* When studying together, you are welcome to watch the teen girls' or women's videos. The women's videos provide longer teachings from Priscilla, but the teen girl videos are edited down to provide more time for discussion and conversation with your daughter. Please note that in the women's version of the videos there will occasionally be a reference to women and moms that would not be found in the teen girl version of the videos, but nothing you would need to review ahead of time.

## STUDY

As you both work through your individual Bible study books, you will discover that the teen girls' version will be shortened. This means you may learn about something that she didn't get to in hers, so we encourage you to share anything that stands out to you as you study the text.

## CONNECT WITH HER

• Plan days to work on personal study together to keep each other accountable.

• Be open with your daughter throughout the week about things you learn or have questions about. Provide a safe place for her to do the same.

• Don't stress! Some weeks will be easier than others to accomplish the personal study days. Just keep pressing forward and making it a priority to meet together each week regardless of how much personal study work was actually done.

## FAQ

*Q:* How old does my teen need to be for this study?

*A:* This study is recommended for girls ages 11 and up.

*Q:* Do I have to purchase the women's videos, or can I use the teen girls' videos to watch with my daughter?

*A:* You can watch either the women's or teen girls' videos with your daughter. It's up to you! The teen girls' videos have been slightly edited with the teen audience in mind.

*Q:* Are there other studies I can do with my teen after this study is over?

*A:* Yes! Many of our studies have both women's and girls' materials available. Check it out at lifeway.com/girls.

### WEEK ONE

1. F. B. Meyer, *The F. B. Meyer Collection, Elijah and the Secret of His Power*, chapter 1.

2. "Yehovah," Strong's H3068, *Blue Letter Bible* online. Available at www.blueletterbible.org.

### WEEK TWO

1. "Cherith," *Holman Bible Dictionary* (Nashville, TN: Holman Bible Publishers, 1991), 247.

2. "Wadi," *Holman Bible Dictionary*, 1398.

3. Ray Pritchard, *Fire and Rain: The Wild-Hearted Faith of Elijah* (Nashville: B&H Publishing, 2007), 55.

4. Gene A. Getz, *Men of Character: Elijah: Remaining Steadfast Through Uncertainty* (Nashville: B&H, 1995), 36.

### WEEK THREE

1. "Zarephath," *Holman Bible Dictionary*, 1433

### WEEK FOUR

1. "Pacach," Strong's H6452, *Blue Letter Bible* online. Available at www.blueletterbible.org.

2. Terence E. Fretheim, *First and Second Kings* (Louisville, KY: Westminster Jon Knox Press, 1999), 102.

3. R. B. Coote (ed.), *Elijah and Elisha in Socioliterary Perspective* (Atlanta: Society of Biblical Literature, 2003), 10.

### WEEK FIVE

1. Tasha Cobbs, "Fill Me Up," UMG on behalf of Motown Gospel, 2016, https://www.youtube.com/watch?v=OKWkYxikygQ.

2. Elisabeth Elliot, *The Path of Loneliness* (Grand Rapids, MI: Revell, 1998), 153.

3. *The F. B. Meyer Collection, Elijah*, chapter 8.

4. F. E. Marsh, *Emblems of the Holy Spirit* (Grand Rapids, MI: Kregel, 1981), 114-115

### WEEK SIX

1. Jeff Lucas, *Elijah: Anointed and Stressed* (Eastbourne, UK: Kingsway Publications, 1995), 121.

# NOTES

# NOTES

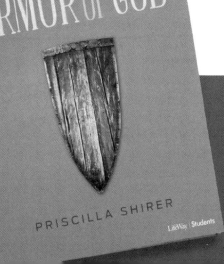

# Get the most from your study.

Customize your Bible study time with a guided experience and additional resources.

Every serious believer longs to summon up the kind of boldness and faith that can stand firm on Mount Carmel and pray down heaven into impossible situations. Yet few are willing to go through the process required to get them there. Strength of faith, character, and boldness can only be shaped in the hidden fires of silence, sameness, solitude, and adversity. Those who patiently wait on God in the darkness always emerge with their loyalty, courage, and belief in Him set afire.

Join Priscilla Shirer on this 7-session journey through the life and times of the prophet Elijah to discover how the fire on Mount Carmel was forged in the valley of famine. Because the emboldened, fiery faith you desire is being fashioned by God in your life at this very moment.

Lifeway designs trustworthy experiences that fuel ministry. Today, the ministries of Lifeway reach more than 160 countries around the globe. For specific information on Lifeway Girls, visit lifeway.com/girls.

## ADDITIONAL RESOURCES

**ELIJAH TEEN GIRLS LEADER KIT**

A 7-session study for teen girls on the story of Elijah. (9781087746913)

**ELIJAH TEEN GIRLS GROUP VIDEO BUNDLE**

The videos for a 7-session study for teen girls on the story of Elijah. (9781087756561)

**ELIJAH FOR WOMEN**
A 7-session, video driven study for Women (9781087715421)
Digital: (9781087738130)